Peony rockii
and
Gansu Mudan

Will McLewin
Dezhong Chen

Wellesley-Cambridge Press

Peony rockii and Gansu Mudan

Printed in the United Kingdom of Great Britain and Northern Ireland

ISBN 0-9614088-3-9

British Library Cataloguing in Publication Data
McLewin, Will
Peony rockii and Gansu Mudan
1. Peonies
I.Title II.Chen, Dezhong
635.9'3362

A catalogue record for this book is available from the British Library

Published in 2006 by Wellesley-Cambridge Press

Box 812060
Wellesley MA 02482 USA
www.wellesleycambridge.com
gs@math.mit.edu

42 Bunkers Hill
Romiley, Stockport, SK6 3DS UK
www.phedar.com
mclewin@phedar.com

Designed by Matthias Thomsen and Will McLewin
Set by Matthias Thomsen

Printed by Handleys Print Solutions
125 Stockport Road West
Bredbury SK6 2BR UK
(0044) (0)161 430 8188

PREFACE

This book is about a group of shrubby peonies, Gansu Mudan, that are still relatively unknown and somewhat mysterious although they are becoming popular and more readily available. There would be little point in it if their appearance was unexceptional and their cultivation difficult, but the reverse is true. They are undemanding in their requirements and are magnificent and spectacular flowering shrubs.

In writing about them we have three aims. The first is to make clear the wide range of forms and colours that exist, to give the correct names of individual cultivars and to explain that they are easy to grow successfully. In short to demystify them and in doing so to establish Gansu Mudan as the correct name for them as a group, with *Paeonia* Gansu Group as their formal collective name.

The second aim is to record that the creation of this group of plants is almost entirely due to the inspiration and effort of one man, Chen Dezhong, and to celebrate his achievement in developing a versatile and hugely significant new group of woody peonies that are without doubt destined to become widespread and rightly very popular.

The third aim is to provide an accurate account of the hybrid plants loosely known as 'Rock's peony', to make clear that they are examples of Gansu Mudan and in doing so separate them from the true wild species plant *P. rockii*.

At the same time, by giving more attention to the general question of names and the use of common terms we hope to raise awareness of such matters and encourage greater care and precision in their use.

Paeonia Gansu Group 'Bing Shan Xue Lian'

冰山雪莲

CONTENTS

INTRODUCTION 1

It may seem perverse to begin a book with chapters of rather difficult prose on what might seem to be arcane topics and with equally arcane discussion of what might seem to be perfectly familiar words (likewise an introduction). As accurate names and correct usage of them is an important part of this book, the beginning is the logical place to put the relevant chapters, and in any case we do not expect anybody to get to grips with Section 1 or even Chapter 1 before looking at pictures in Section 3. We have no concerns about including sentences and extended passages that need to be read twice or several times for their meaning and purpose to be clear. We are happy to trust the reader to do that and not to be put off. Frequently, for clarification or to avoid an implication that is not intended, parenthetical qualifying additions have to be made, either in brackets or between commas, in sentences that are already long. The previous sentence to this one is an example. Omitting them at a second reading and then putting them back will often be helpful.

The three main sections are very different in style and content and can be regarded as independent of each other. Certainly each could exist, in different contexts, without the other two. The same is true to some extent of individual Chapters. To help this stand alone aspect of the different parts there is a bit of repetition, here and there, of some information. As by far the greater part of information in this book is not culled from other sources but is first hand experience of the authors the usual list of references is absent. Where we think some are necessary or helpful they appear at the ends of the chapters concerned.

We know only part of the whole picture of course. This does not distinguish us from other authors, but we are at least aware of it and conscious that the most important thing to know is what you do not know.

There are several minor problems of presentation which are best dealt with here.

It is traditional to use an italic font for what are called scientific names of plants. 'Scientific' is somewhat inappropriate because plant classification and naming, although it increasingly uses modern science and technology, is not very scientific, possibly for perfectly good reasons. 'Scientific' in this context really means formal, or 'not common', or universal, this last being the crucial point. 'Scientific' names (in botany) are made universal by restricting them to Latin. As this is a 'dead' language not used anywhere for everyday communication this seems to us distinction enough and we are not aware of any ambiguity that would result from not writing them in italic. Nevertheless, for the most part we adhere to this convention. There are other conventions that we have not followed. Most readers will not notice their absence; those that do will have no difficulty coping without them, which seems to us reason enough for not adhering to them.

Another occasional problem occurs where an everyday word has been given a special meaning in botanical nomenclature. Here it is 'group'. Botanical nomenclaturists will point out that the upper case G distinguishes a 'group of plants' from a 'plant Group'. We hope that our comments in Chapter 1 will not make matters worse.

Chinese words or at least their *pinyin* version are also somewhat problematic. Pinyin is the modern, official way to transcribe (or represent) Chinese in the Latin alphabet. Official in the sense both of formally designated and approved by the Chinese government for general purposes on the one hand, and by the International Codes of Plant Nomenclature for plant names on the other.

The literal meaning of pinyin is 'spell sound'. It supersedes the earlier Wade-Giles scheme. The question arises of whether to delineate pinyin words by any or all of italics or single quote marks or initial letters in uppercase. We do sometimes.

As we point out in Chapter1 the pinyin expression 'mudan' is preferable to 'tree peony' and we use it throughout. We use 'the West' rather loosely, usually to mean parts or all of North America and Europe in contrast to China.

Chinese names (of people) even in their transliterated pinyin form create a dilemma. In China they are written and spoken family name first and given names second. Chinese authors of papers in scientific journals and increasingly in general publications in the West are more-or-less obliged to adopt the convention, not entirely consistent, of given name, or initials, first and family name second. Our compromise here is to use the same order for the authors' names on the cover and in the formal information about the book, but in the contents to write Chinese names as they would be written in China. Thus Chen Dezhong is Dezhong Chen on the cover etc but is always Chen Dezhong in the body of the book and his daughter Fuhui is always Chen Fuhui. This, incidentally reveals another usage custom. Dezhong and Fuhui, for example, are both two one-syllable pinyin words, the most common form of given names, but they are usually written and used as if they were a single two syllable word. However when given names in pinyin are abbreviated to initials both are used, Chen, D. Z. or D. Z. Chen for example.

和平二乔

Paeonia Gansu Group 'He Ping Er Qiao'

MC 2005

INTRODUCTION 2

Although two names only appear as authors this book is, to a considerable extent, a collaborative endeavour by all the people in it. Help and advice has been freely and generously given and it is a great pleasure for us to acknowledge this. The presiding spirit has been the celebration of Gansu Mudan and our affection for, our delight in, and our excitement with these plants, emotions that characterise the work on them at the three nurseries involved. The feeling of cooperating in something bigger than all of us has been profound, indeed moving at times and a great pleasure to be part of.

We are indeed fortunate and delighted that the book is graced with wonderful paintings by Margaret Walty which, while being botanically accurate in minute detail, have also captured a hint of traditional Chinese paintings of peonies.

The photographs, with a few exceptions, have not been taken specifically for use in the book. Rather they have been chosen from 'the photographs we have'. A few are not particularly good examples of photographs but that does not matter, they are adequate to illustrate and add to and illuminate the text. Most have been taken by Chen Fuhui, a lot by Coralie Christiani and some by Will McLewin, Chen Dezhong, Robert Pardo and Hu Xiaoling. Some of the information comes from Chen Dezhong's little book (in Chinese) on Ziban Mudan. There are a few places where other sources are involved that are obvious and acknowledged but the vast majority of the information is pooled first hand experience of people in the book. This is not a book trawled from other accounts and articles and other people's experience or, in its absence, their assumptions. Chapter 5 is a reminder of the perils of that approach. That chapter took a long time and would have been much less complete without the painstaking investigative work contributed by Chris Sanders. Our cooperation with him to determine the truth about 'Rock's peony became an adventure, both exciting and frustrating in turn, and involved many earnest discussions about, in some cases, ever smaller points of detail or their implications. Hu Xiaoling and Chen Fuhui made major contributions to assembling and organising the contents, responding promptly and patiently whenever help was needed.

On the practical side of actually producing the book we found again generous help from friends. We greatly appreciate Professor Gil Strang's willingness to have this book sitting alongside his erudite and illuminating mathematics texts at Wellesley-Cambridge Press. We expected that producing the final computer discs for printing would be troublesome and stressful. Instead Matthias Thomsen designed and produced the elegant version that you see swiftly and calmly.

A source of encouragement throughout was the assurance of another friend, Roger Handley, who said from the beginning that the actual printing could be safely left in his hands and he was right. After some considerable complications with assembling parts of the contents, to have the last two stages accomplished with such panache and expertise was a truly joyful experience.

Alf Coombs, Andy Firth, Jack Garside, Nigel Titley, Andy Johnson and others listed at the end of Chapter 5 all provided bits of help at different times. So too did Irmtraud and Gottlob Rieck whose consistent encouragement we are glad to acknowledge. Irmtraud and Gottlob are largely responsible for *Strauchpfingstrosen* (2002), Ulmer, the best general book on mudan that we know of, but inexplicably still available only in German.

Errors, omissions and infelicities are our responsibility.

Will McLewin and Chen Dezhong,
Stockport and Lanzhou, 2006

墨
海
银
波

Paeonia Gansu Group 'Mo Hai Yin Bo'

NAMES AND HISTORY

---

1. THE QUESTION OF NAMES

Plants (like people) have innate physical characteristics but do not intrinsically have names. People give plants names for their own purposes, most importantly for meaningful discussion and exchange of information, also in some cases for self-gratification. Misuse or careless use of names defeats their purpose and renders them useless or worse, but what constitutes misuse is, in many cases, itself controversial. This book is about a particular group of cultivated mudan (shrubby peonies) for which the appropriate common name, in our view, is Gansu Mudan and the formal name we propose is *Paeonia* Gansu Group. A basic problem when discussing objects or accounts of events that have been widely incorrectly described is that many of the names involved have been corrupted by their misuse but nevertheless have still to be used. Consequently, before individual plants in this group and the group as a whole can

be presented and their origins, virtues, characteristics and availability described it is necessary to discuss various names and terms used and to explain the position of these plants in the context of mudan in general.

1.1 Paeonia
The genus *Paeonia* as a whole is uncontroversial in the sense that there are no serious disputes or problems about which of the earth's and of humanity's plants are peonies. *Paeonia* was formerly included in the family *Ranunculaceae* but is now the sole member of the family *Paeoniaceae*. Within *Paeonia* there are two well-defined main sections (and the unnecessary small third section for the two very similar North American herbaceous species). One section consists of peonies with permanent over-wintering woody stems. The common name is 'tree peonies', which is misleading because they are much more shrubs than trees. The name used by botanists for this

section is Moutan, an early transliteration from Chinese for the compound character now spelled Mudan in pinyin. The established, unambiguous and modern Chinese pinyin word Mudan is easy to say* and to spell. We use it throughout and recommend its use generally. (Incidentally, and usefully, 'mudan' is both singular and plural. See 9.2). The other section consists of herbaceous peonies, with non-woody stems which do not over-winter and grow anew each year, The pinyin word for these plants is Shaoyao. (There are some details about the origin of these Chinese terms in Chapter 4.) In the last few decades an intermediate section of Itoh or intersectional peonies has been developed, initially by crossing examples of mudan with examples of shaoyao. These peonies have blurred the distinction between the two main sections and as more examples are produced the once simple morphological distinction will be obscured by examples of intersectional hybrids which are not clearly intermediate but very close to one section or the other.

---

* (Consonants as in English; mu long as in 'moon'; dan short, like 'can' and with a slight stress.)

1.2 Gansu Mudan and Paeonia Gansu Group; 'rockii hybrids'

With mudan as the term for woody peonies in general the immediate question that needs comment is why Gansu Mudan or Gansu Group is the most appropriate name to use for this group or subset of woody peonies a whole. Perversely we begin by explaining why alternative names that have been used are inappropriate. The (wild) species now called *Paeonia rockii* is definitely the ancestral species most prominently involved and genetic material from *P. rockii* is undoubtedly present, albeit in almost all cases not directly. In addition, the plants themselves exhibit several of the properties that characterise *P. rockii,* most notably the dark blotch at the base of the flower petals and the vigour and tough versatility of *P. rockii*. Perhaps 'P. rockii hybrids' would seem an obvious choice for the group as a whole. However the word hybrid carries with it certain implications which do not necessarily apply here, particularly when it comes attached to a (wild) species name. (The use of the terms 'species' and 'hybrid' is discussed in Chapter 2).

If some plants are produced by crossing a true plant of *P. rockii* with another peony, say *P. xx* it is reasonable to describe them as P. rockii hybrids (describing is not the same as naming). Of course it is equally appropriate to describe them as P. *xx* hybrids. (It can be argued that which of *P. rockii* and *P. xx* is the female parent should determine how their offspring are named but there is neither agreement about nor general usage of this convention and in any case it is not helpful here.) Most Gansu Mudan are not *P. rockii* hybrids in this precise sense. If subsequently a P. rockii hybrid in this precise sense is crossed with *P. xx* are the resulting plants still *P. rockii* hybrids? And so on. Like most groups of cultivated plants of hybrid origin Gansu Mudan include hybrids of hybrids of hybrids ……, with many plants of both known and unknown identity involved. (This analysis explains why a name of the form '<genus name> <species name> hybrids' is unsatisfactory in any genus and why it is not allowed in the current rules for plant nomenclature. See also below.) A further complication discussed in more detail in Chapter 3 is that what *P. rockii* itself is or is not is a far from simple question, especially in the context of past use in hybridisation.

There is a great deal of inaccurate (or worse) and misleading nomenclature involved with this group of plants. Frequently if they are white or pale pink they are called *P. rockii* for the prestige of this name when, of course, they are simply not species *P. rockii*. Or they are called something like '*Paeonia* Joseph Rock' or 'Rock's Peony' which is (almost always) incorrect for reasons explained in Chapter 5.

Using the Chinese province of Gansu for the name of this group of plants is both accurate and appropriate and has no misleading connotations. True *P. rockii* is found in other provinces, Sichuan and Shanxi for example but Gansu is where it is mainly found.

Additionally, although Gansu Mudan are now widely distributed in China and there have been examples from ancient times the emergence of the present cultivars as a major new group is effectively due to the work of Chen Dezhong at Peace Peony Nursery in central Gansu.

The term Gansu Mudan was first proposed in 1992 by Professor Li Jaijue of Lanzhou University as a more precise name than the familiar (in China) but imprecise name Ziban Mudan. This last name represents all mudan with flowers that have purple (or dark) blotches and includes the wild species (both the distinct-or-not forms of *P. rockii* and others and the doubtful *P. yananensis*), those Central Plains or suffruticosa hybrids that have dark blotches and the mudan cultivars developed by Chen Dezhong. Gansu Mudan as a name, both collective and individual, has several advantages from a Western point of view. It is short, easy to spell and to say and unlike many names for plants of non-Western origin that have been given Western names this name honours the Chinese origin of the plants. So we propose the simple unambiguous elegance of Gansu Mudan for the plants, with *Paeonia* Gansu Group as the group name for formal taxonomic purposes.

(For people who enjoy this sort of thing we should point out that strictly, what is proposed here is *Paeonia* Gansu Cultivar Group, a collective name for an assemblage of individual cultivars (sharing some particular characteristic or characteristics) although the word 'Cultivar' is not formally included in the name. However the term cultivar itself allows "an assemblage" of plants (sharing some particular characteristic or characteristics) and the term 'Group' is sometimes used to make explicit the assemblage that is allowed under a single cultivar name. Crucially 'Cultivar', and 'Cultivar Group' both allow inclusion of unnamed (or named) plants that have arisen or will arise in the future with the appropriate characteristics. There is a basic problem here that essentially comes from the difference between the definition of the concept and the definition of what can be recognised as a legitimately published example. Since the word 'group' has a well-known meaning as an everyday word the distinction between 'group' and 'Group' is crucial. It is perhaps unkind to say that a Group of plants is a group of plants that has been validly named as a Plant Group.)

From the point of view of the formal validity of the name *Paeonia* Gansu Group according to the International Code of Nomenclature for Cultivated Plants four questions or comments arise. Something like *Paeonia rockii* hybrids cannot legitimately or sensibly be used as explained above. The use of 'Gansu' has occurred previously, possibly without all the formal details some would desire but if there were doubts about

whether it has been unambiguously proposed and validly published they are hereby now resolved. The genus name or a transliteration of it cannot be used as part of the name because it involves a tautology. *Paeonia* Gansu Group avoids that problem but nobody should be expected to say of a plant "This [woody] peony belongs to the *Paeonia* Gansu Group". "It is a Gansu Mudan" or "They are Gansu Mudan" is so much simpler. When a plant group name is coined initially, the extant members are not always clearly defined, and as more plants are produced there will always be some ambiguity or uncertainty about whether particular plants are members of a particular group. This is not in itself a fatal flaw provided the concept is reasonably clear and the name meets what should be the most important criterion which is to be useful and helpful. Gansu Mudan, the plants that comprise or should be assigned to *Paeonia* Gansu Group, in one sense define themselves but they are described or delineated in more detail in Chapter 4, by their properties in Section 2 and by their pictures in Section 3.

The contrast between Gansu Mudan and the well-known shrubby peonies, suffruticosa hybrids, is instructive here as in other places. *P. suffruticosa*, until fairly recently, was an example of the insistence in horticulture/botany of persisting with mistakes in initial publications and nomenclatural designations. *P. suffruticosa* was described (by Western botanists) as a species of peony on the basis of an imported plant which was actually and definitely a cultivated hybrid. Recently the name *P. spontanaea* has been partially accepted as the valid (ie first legitimately published) name for the ancestral species from which the suffruticosa hybrids were most prominently (supposedly) derived. (There is a complication with a more recently designated species name, *P. jishanensis*, see Chapter 2.) If *P. suffruticosa* had ever been appropriate as a species name and was still a valid name then the objections outlined above to using it for a group of cultivated hybrids would apply with equal force, but now that the familiar, and in some sense established, name *P. suffruticosa* has been shown not to represent a true, wild species it becomes at least an acceptable candidate as the name for that group of hybrids. (Except of course that 'suffruticosa hybrids' is formally unacceptable and for most people obliged to use it unnecessarily awkward to say and to spell and meaningless.) All that said, the Chinese name for those plants is Zhongyuan Mudan meaning central plains woody peonies (hybrids) and this would be a more appropriate name, but it is awkward for Western ears and suffruticosa is probably too entrenched to change. Whatever would be most appropriate, it is not our concern here, although when we need to refer to them we will usually call them Central Plains hybrids

1.3 *Paeonia rockii*

There is no doubt whatsoever that there are populations of wild Mudan with certain characteristics (bi-pinnate leaves with several to many small leaflets, white-petaled flowers with a dark basal blotch, etc.) for which an identifying species name is appropriate. Unfortunately the introduction of 'rockii' in the designation of *P. suffruticosa* ssp *rockii* by Haw and Lauener in 1990 compounded the error inherent in *P. suffruticosa* and involved a false premise. It was, in a large part, based on a cultivated hybrid/intermediate (the Highdown plant, see Chapter 5) and a poor herbarium specimen with no field data to support it and it was (and is still) impossible to determine to which wild plants this new name then applied. It is entirely appropriate that Chinese botanists proposed the epithet *P. rockii* based on true wild plants, or to put this another way, that the wild mudan involved were regarded as an independent species (raised to specific status). Incidentally, it is only fair to point out that Li Jiajue had already said that this change was necessary in his first book on purple-blotched mudan in 1988. To add to the confusion there are (or at least were) some plants resulting from seed sent by J. F. Rock in 1925 which came from plants in cultivation. While it is **conceivable** that the seed was true *P. rockii* seed contrary alternatives seem to us more plausible. Such questions in general may be answerable with molecular analysis but in this particular case this is now impossible. There are very few plants for which there is actual evidence that they germinated from Rock's seed and as we explain in Chapter 5 they are Gansu Mudan and not true *P. rockii*. Other examples we know of labelled P. 'Joseph Rock ' or something similar

and seedlings propagated from them are also not *P. rockii* but simply examples of Gansu Mudan.

More recently there has been considerable field work by Chinese botanists and much more and more precise information is available. Unfortunately the Chinese botanists involved have not yet arrived at a consistent consensual formulation, so their valuable work has not yet resulted in a clear picture nor with a set of names which can easily and accurately be applied. The elements which contribute to the complexity of the situation can be separated into two types. Some are familiar to taxonomists, namely, the extent to which species status depends on morphology only (ie appearance) or on phylogeny (ie parentage etc.) or on a mixture of the two. The interaction of these two ideas determines the extent to which different populations are lumped together under a single species name and the extent to which plants of unknown origin can be given an established species name because the appearance of all of them fits within a published description, and on the other hand the extent to which plants of varied appearance can be given the same species name because they are all present in a wild population. Also uncertain is the degree of morphological distinction required for different species or subspecies designation. Such questions are settled in practice by the acceptance or not of a particular taxonomic proposal or scheme. At present there is no consensus but Hong Deyuan's fairly recent revision of the genus paeonia in China published in Flora of China will probably lead to this becoming basically the accepted scheme irrespective of the merits or this or other schemes and in spite of more recent revisions by Hong Deyuan. There is some agreement that there are two forms of wild 'rockii-type' plants, initially called *P. rockii* and *P. rockii* ssp *linyanshani* by Hong Tao et al but now called *P. rockii* ssp *rockii* and *P. rockii* ssp *taibaishanica* by Hong Deyuan et al (but the other way round) The difference between the two is in the lobing or not of the leaflets. The form most common in the wild, Hong Deyaun's *P. rockii* ssp. *rockii*, has mostly unlobed leaflets, although the size and number of leaflets varies considerably between populations (see Chapter 3). (These plants were called *P. rockii* ssp.*linyanshani* by Hong Tao because in the paper by Haw and Lauener that raised some purple-blotch peonies (although it is unclear which) to sub-species status as *P. suffruticosa* ssp. *rockii* their illustrative leaf diagram was of a cultivated hybrid with lobed leaves.) They now seem likely to remain *P. rockii* ssp. *rockii*. This classification, largely accepted at present, is in fact much less clear-cut than the various papers and authors supporting it imply and is discussed in more detail in Chapter 3.

In addition to these, perhaps academic, considerations there are further problems. Mudan has been the subject of intensive cultivation and breeding for many centuries, long before the current approaches to classification were established. That most wild populations are now remnant relics increases difficulties but is not itself a great problem. (At least not for 'rockii-type' mudan. For *P. spontanaea* and so-called *P. ostii* it seems to us it is a severe problem because the existence of authentic wild ancestral plants is very doubtful.) A much bigger problem for the taxonomy of wild Mudan arises from the long-established use of the root bark (*danpi*) as a medicine. The fact that danpi has a monetary value has meant not only that wild plants have been collected and destroyed but that Mudan have been planted in wild places, so that the truly wild nature of some Mudan is doubtful and impossible to ascertain. This is particularly the case with some plants in Yanan, Shanxi Province where there are several interesting examples, for some of which some botanists have proposed specific status. There are also wild rockii- type plants with pink and purple-pink coloured flowers. Without careful analysis and compelling evidence to the contrary there is no justification in regarding such plants as other than Gansu Mudan and the direct or indirect result of human activity. Classification difficulties in no way detract from the splendour and horticultural value of the plants involved but in our view they increase the need for an appropriately designated name, namely Gansu Mudan (formally *Paeonia* Gansu Group) for the group of cultivated hybrid plants involved and make it imperative that the name *P. rockii* is not applied to plants without appropriate wild provenance.

1.4 Ziban Mudan

In China, this term is applied to all mudan that have dark blotches or marks at the base of the petals irrespective of the colour of the blotch and the petals and of the identity and origins of the plant. Thus a central plains hybrid with dark basal blotches, presumably the result of the presence of genetic material from a rockii-type plant, could be called a Ziban Mudan. Additionally the two species or doubtful species or 'wild hybrids' or 'hybrids, once cultivated, found in the wild' *P. yananensis* and P. *baokangensis* are Ziban Mudan. Consequently the term Ziban Mudan is not exactly equivalent to the term Gansu Mudan or to *P. rockii* (whatever that name means). The term/expression/word Ziban itself is misunderstood in the West due to a rather simplistic translation. It is the case that zi is the word in Chinese for purple but it is also used in this context to mean simply 'dark'. The plants to which the term Ziban Mudan is applied include a wide range of blotch colour from darkish red through purple to black and in fact the most common blotch colour in Gansu Mudan and their wild *P. rockii* ancestors is black. In passing we note that some of the plants in cultivation described as P. 'Rock's Variety' or something similar have purple or purplish blotches, casting further doubt (although none is needed) on the validity of their being true species plants. (It is immediately clear from the pictures of Gansu Mudan in section 3 that blotch colour is not a simple matter.) There is no doubt that the development of Gansu Mudan (or the *Paeonia* Gansu Group) as a whole has involved true wild plants collected by Chen Dezhong, but also Ziban Mudan used in the sense so that the term *P. rockii* hybrids while undoubtedly having a desirable cachet to Western horticulturists and gardeners is inappropriate.

1.5 Names of cultivated hybrids

There is considerable confusion about English language names for individual Gansu Mudan varieties, where there should be none. Simple adoption of the pinyin transliteration of the Chinese character name is the designated valid approach and is greatly preferable to the incorrect practice of choosing Western names for commercial purposes. Using the pinyin version of the Chinese name is straightforward and legitimate and requires only that the remaining inherent reluctance to do so be overcome. To encourage this appropriate approach we have given this topic more attention than is usually the case, see Sections 3 and 4. Of course for a genuinely new cultivar or an established clone without a validly published name (see Chapter 5) different considerations apply. There are also complications arising from the use of Western colour names and the much more general question of accurate identification, discussed in chapters 9.1 and 9.3.

Apart from these questions about the cultivar or variety name one thing that is clear is that the word 'rockii' should not be a part of it. If the cultivar name is, say, Hong Lian then the correct name for the plant is *Paeonia* 'Hong Lian' or Peony 'Hong Lian'. Peony rockii 'Hong Lian' is invalid and incorrect because Gansu Mudan are not selections from true *P. rockii*.

It may be helpful to point out here that the International Code of Nomenclature for Cultivated Plants explicitly allows in cultivar names both the latin form and the common name of a genus, so *Paeonia* and Peony are both valid and are to be regarded as equivalent.

Gansu Mudan at Peace Peony Nursery

2.   A BASIC OVERVIEW OF MUDAN CULTIVAR GROUPS AND WILD MUDAN SPECIES

Before discussing mudan species and hybrid groups it is necessary to review some of the terms involved and to point out that this is not intended as an in-depth academic discussion, but to provide enough basic clarification to render the remarks about mudan categories useful and unambiguous and to increase insight through awareness of the difficulties instead of, as is often the case, increasing misunderstanding by glossing over them.

By species plants we always mean wild plants whose form and characteristics are the result of natural evolution uninfluenced by human intervention in any direct sense. By cultivated plants or groups of cultivars or hybrid groups we mean plants that do not naturally occur in the wild and whose existence is the result of human activity, deliberate or otherwise. For cultivated plants the term Group now has a formal meaning roughly equivalent to that of species for wild plants. While each of these concepts is simple neither is completely easy to use in practice. Among botanists, and horticulturists and media people who write or comment on such matters everyone knows what is meant by a species but there is no agreed definition and everyone knows something different to everyone else. Bear in mind that wild plants are not intrinsically divided into different sets, each called a species. In practice a particular set of plants is a species if botanists/botanical taxonomists on the whole agree or at least accept that it is. This bizarre situation can easily be defended and certainly has substantial advantages but it is at the same time profoundly unsatisfactory. Perhaps we should say it is profoundly unsatisfactory to a scientific frame of mind but uncontroversial to, say, a theological frame of mind. At the heart of the problem is the question of whether species is a phylogenic concept (ie determined by parentage/ancestry) or a morphological concept (ie determined by appearance). In many cases the two do more-or-less coincide, which, paradoxically at first sight, is largely why there is a problem.

Most formal definitions of the species concept involve phylogeny much more than morphology, but almost all classification (formal definitions of different species) is done in terms of morphology, for fairly obvious reasons. Comparisons with animals are misleading: for familiar animals the idea of species is more like the idea of genus in (familiar) plants. For higher levels of classification there is only rarely controversy; most plant genera are defined quite well by morphological characters and in most cases members of one genus will not breed with members of another. Also for lower levels of classification, such as form, the criteria are simply morphological and often not maintained in offspring.

In between the extreme and well-defined examples of wild plants and cultivated plants there is a large complicated grey area. Of course a wild species plant that is collected and grown in a garden remains the same wild species plant. If it then produces seed the plants grown from that seed should generally not be properly regarded as true examples of the species in question (unless the species is apomictic). In practice they will almost always be labelled with the species name either innocently or because the seed has been produced for commercial reasons but they will almost always not be true examples of the species but cultivated hybrids as they result from fertilisation of the true species plant (determined by its provenance!) by pollen from another plant which is not a true species plant. There is scope in cultivation for rigorously ensuring that a true species plant is fertilised only by another such plant but this is rarely what happens. In such cases and of course in a wild population the offspring may not be homogeneous in appearance and may not exactly resemble either of the parents but they are by definition part of the species population and are part of its morphological diversity. The appearance (morphological) of offspring is, in a sense, irrelevant because when plants from two different (accepted) species are crossed some or all of the offspring may look exactly or more-or-less like one of the parents or like an example of a third (accepted) species. A further complication quite often occurs when 'species' plants are grown from seed in cultivation. Assume that the original parent plants are true examples of the species and there is persistent and rigorous prevention of external fertilisation. If extreme examples are repeatedly selected (that exhibit some particular feature or colour for example) then although all can be regarded as true species plants successive generations become increasingly unrepresentative of the wild population that defines the species. Indeed rather few generations may be needed to produce examples that cannot be (or at least have not been) found as wild plants and which do not satisfy the morphological description of the species. An exactly parallel problem arises with a named cultivated plant. Its offspring from seed will in most cases vary and differ from the parent whether it is self-pollinated or not. The extent to which such offspring can properly be labelled with the cultivar name or cultivar group name depends to some extent on how the name has been defined but in most cases the offspring should not be given the parent name. Almost always of course they are, in both cases. It is perhaps unkind to point out that the detailed and complex (and admirable) rules on plant nomenclature which define whether or not any particular name for a species or a cultivar group can be valid nowhere involve a definition of the two concepts, but necessary because no outsider would believe such a thing.

The word hybrid is widely used and its meaning assumed to be clear. It is nevertheless a problematic concept and is generally used in an unhelpfully loose way, particularly when a name is attached to it. The implication is that two plants with differences in genetic make-up have combined sexually (by whatever means) to produce offspring, and because the parents are genetically different the offspring as a whole will be a mixture of and different to both. Some plants are self-infertile (there is evidence that (some at least) mudan are) so that seed can only be produced by two genetically different parents and so in a sense all resulting offspring must be hybrids. However when the parents are both from the same species (the implication being that there are sufficient genetic differences for fertilisation but not enough to render them different species) then the offspring are not hybrids but more members of the same species. This leads to perhaps the most common element of definitions of the species concept, that its members breed true within the prescribed limits of morphological variation. This satisfying idea is routinely abused in practice because the limits are necessarily defined by the wild population(s) and botanists are rarely able to do sufficient fieldwork to accurately determine them. Most cultivar plants are hybrids in the sense that they result from seed where not both the parents are true examples of the same species although some are simply exceptional/abnormal selections from species plants. Most have very complex ancestry and are hybrids of hybrids of hybrids… . Two further observations add to the complexity of the situation. A truly wild plant will usually be referred to or regarded as a hybrid if its appearance is intermediate between that of two (designated/accepted) species. Its hybrid origin is actually an historical event that is assumed but not known and even if somehow the 'cross-fertilisation' could be established the term hybrid only follows because the two parents are regarded as members of different species. The current practice (unchanged since Linnaeus 1707-1778!) is to assign such plants to one or other of the two species or to a new species or to argue that the existence of such plants necessitates the combining of the two species to one with a broader morphological range. Much the same applies to cultivated 'hybrids' albeit with slightly different 'parameters'. A general adoption of the term 'intermediate' both as a description and as a designation and much more careful and restricted use of the term 'hybrid' would have much to recommend it. Accurate, as opposed to merely confident, use of all the concepts involved requires knowledge of the immediate and distant history of the plants involved and for most plants that most people encounter this is absent and rarely remedied by the attachment of a label. In practice the term 'hybrid plant' effectively means 'not a (wild) species plant', which is not really the same thing. Offspring of a self-fertile parent may be hybrids in one sense (for example if the parent is itself, for the sake of argument, a hybrid) and may well have varied morphology but are not hybrids the in the sense defined above. In many cases the name adopted involves a species name and this makes already unsatisfactory conventional usage worse because the involvement of the species cited may be either many generations earlier or simply erroneous. As there is no accepted term other than hybrid to imply 'not a true species plant' in the sense we have defined it and as certain groups of plants are known as so-and-so hybrids we are obliged to make use of the term.

The complications outlined above with what are superficially simple but actually very complex concepts apply in varying degrees to most plant genera. With the mudan section of paeonia they are compounded by three extra factors, one of which is unique to mudan.

The first is that Western (and some Chinese) botanists have defined species and coined names for them with very little background information and experience and little or no field-work, and in most cases based on single or very few specimens often dried and in herbaria some of which were in fact cultivated hybrids. *P. papaveracea* and *P. suffruticosa* are the classic examples in the present context. This has been standard practice and continues today. Where the plants involved are obscure and come from homogeneous populations it is, perhaps, defensible and may well be helpful. In the case of mudan the plants have been deeply involved in and cultivated in a civilisation much older than that of the western botanists and the consequence has been endless inaccuracy and confusion. There are more details of the basic history and the errors outlined in Chapter 3, and on so-called 'Rock's peony' in Chapter 5.

The second involves more recent studies. Chinese botanists have investigated wild mudan and the origins and characteristics of cultivated hybrids and published many papers with, not unreasonably, only summaries in English. Unfortunately the aggregate of these extensive and very welcome publications, scattered across various academic journals, is characterised by contradictions and competition between eminent authors and by frequent revisions. Chinese botanists have the particular handicap of having to accommodate as best they can the names and taxonomic mess left by earlier Western botanists, and continued in some recently published books. Such comments

could be made about most plant genera endemic to China and are made here as matter of fact and not as derogatory criticism (well, mostly not).

At the present time an agreed accepted overall description of species and hybrid mudan has not been reached but the basic features outlined below seem secure. Further field-work and more extensive molecular studies will undoubtedly lead to further revision but the main elements of the picture presented by, for example, Hong Deyuan in the new Flora of China in 2001 based on morphological studies are likely to prevail if only because this is the most readily accessible and most authoritative reference. This in spite of the fact that he has already since published articles which modify his account there. It is corroborated more-or-less by a subsequent molecular study and does not differ greatly from an earlier survey. For more detailed accounts of the genus than that presented here the five references below, are together perhaps the best starting point and the gateway to many others, and no doubt there are many more to come

The third complication is exceptional and has far-reaching consequences. For hundreds of years the root bark of woody peonies has been a significant element of traditional Chinese medicine. It is called 'danpi'. (Here pi means skin or bark and dan does not mean simply red but signifies something of value.) Unlike, for example, the bark of *Quercus suber* which can be harvested for cork products without killing the tree the root bark of shrubby peonies cannot be harvested easily without destroying the plant. The obvious and actual consequence has been the destruction of many wild shrubby peonies. We are not able to be precise about the extent but it is certainly so great that ancestral species of some hybrid groups are, as far as is known, now essentially non-existent. (See, for example *P. spontanea* below). The implications for mudan taxonomy are obvious and are a significant factor in much of the present confusion and controversy. In places where species mudan once grew there are none and for some species the places where they can still be found are obscure and relatively inaccessible. But another serious consequence of the monetary value of danpi is that mudan have been planted in wild locations by people without their own land. As this would

above left and right: Various forms of *Paeonia delavayi*

generally have been secretive the locations are unknown and the extent to which it has happened impossible to guess. As this practice has likely taken place over the many hundreds of years during which mudan have been gathered from the wild and actively cultivated and hybridised, the inferences that can be drawn from wild populations (particularly small ones) will rarely be as secure as botanists would wish them to be. We should point out that several authors have published confident, eloquent even, revisions of Mudan that do not share our reservations. Such expositions are certainly more comforting (to the uncritical reader) than many of our observations.

With these preliminary observations to be borne in mind we can now present a basic overview of the mudan section of the genus paeonia. Simple alphabetic lists of species names, and even binary keys, are the standard way to describe a genus and an easy option for the writer. However they are less helpful to the reader than they appear to be because they do not provide an insightful overall perspective and their linear nature gives all names equal weight. As the purpose here is not a comprehensive exposition but a basic, pragmatic summary a less formal approach is more appropriate.

While it is crucially important to be and to remain clear about the distinction between wild species plants and cultivated plants the most helpful way to approach mudan as a whole is to begin by separating them, rather crudely, into different groups each consisting of certain species and certain cultivated hybrids, although in truth very little can be described as certain. (Here the term group is used in its general sense and not with the particular meaning defined (well actually not explicitly defined) in the International Code of Nomenclature for Cultivated Plants. It is used there partly to avoid the complications arising from the ambiguous term hybrid.) Also, although there are the four distinct groups of plants outlined below, each centred on a particular species and geographical area, plus a fifth for convenience, this does not mean that every particular woody peony belongs unequivocally to one of them. A direct hybrid between two of the base species could be regarded as belonging to both the corresponding groups. As almost all the hybrid plants have a much more complex, distant and usually unknown, species ancestry each group is an imprecise but nevertheless useful aggregate.

Paeonia ludlowii

Delavayi group

The simplest group conceptually is the complex species or complex of species called Paeonia delavayi and the relatively few cultivated hybrids derived from them. In the past several species or sub-species have been described, again based on relatively few examples. Now the woody peonies that had *potaninii, lutea, trollioides* etc. as part of their name have been subsumed (by some authors) into the greatly variable species *P. delavayi*. Individuals range from a half to two metres in height, with generally small flowers from yellow to black-red. Leaves have generally fewer leaflets than in the other groups but individual leaflets are generally more lobed and dissected. Plants in this group show varying degrees of stolonicity in their growth. In spite of the great differences they are regarded as a single species because most known wild populations are heterogenous with a continuous spectrum of different forms. Another species in this group is *P. ludlowii*, a larger plant. It was previously designated a sub-species of the now subsumed *P. lutea* although it is morphologically and geographically distinct. In China this group of species and forms has not been greatly involved in breeding cultivated varieties, presumably because the flowers are small and probably because they do not cross readily with other groups. This is regrettable because most of

the plants in this group are frost hardy and this character could have been developed in those other groups of hybrids in which are not so reliably hardy. Plants of the *P. delavayi* complex and *P. ludlowii* have been used more in Europe and the United States in the creation of hybrids and although the names recorded for the plants used should be treated with caution this is probably why yellow flowered examples are much more frequent than in the groups of Chinese hybrids. In fact the familiar, *P. ludlowii*, called large yellow mudan in China, regarded as totally hardy in Europe, requires protection to survive the fierce winters of, for example, Lanzhou in Gansu.

Suffruticosa group

The plants of the most familiar group have been known in the West for many years as `P. suffruticosa hybrids'. The name derives from one of the earliest mistakes by Western botanists who coined the species name for a double-flowered cultivated hybrid and the name has caused confusion ever since. Subsequently other mudan, now regarded as distinct species, were assigned the status of sub-species of *P. suffruticosa*. This is the main group of cultivated Chinese mudan and together they represent many hundreds of years of experiment and development. There are now over 1000 named cultivars, which may be forms or clones, and there are many books of selections. ‚Chinese Tree Peony' edited by Wang Lianying is arguably the best. The Chinese name for this group of plants is

Paeonia jishanensis

Paeonia jishanensis

P. jishanensis type without wild provenance; the faint purple pink colour at the base of the petals is more pronounced when the flower first opens.

short mudan in China) which seems now to be accepted as a distinct species and does at least have a Chinese name. It may well be the same as *P. spontanaea* as has been argued, even though it is basically white-flowered and *P. spontanaea* was named for a red-flowered plant, possibly not a true wild plant. This itself is strange because there are old reports of hillsides of red-flowered mudan but none can be found now. Their one-time existence is at least plausible because red (pink through red to claret-purple) is the dominant colour in the Central Plains group. Presumably we have to accept that the wild red-flowered mudan have been collected to extinction. Indications of the involvement of several now-recognised species can be seen in the Central Plains group (and in any group of hybrids) and while indications are not the same as knowledge it is hard to believe that any wild species can have totally avoided making a contribution during the centuries of work on this group.

Feng Dan group

A third group is Feng Dan peonies, also known as the Southern Yangtse group. These plants are the most prolific source of danpi because their roots, although relatively few, are thick and fast growing and with a thick and easily removed root bark. They are cultivated on a vast scale in parts of China south of the Yangtse river for the production of danpi. The plants are morphologically fairly distinct from other mudan and usually white flowered (Feng Dan Bai). The white flowered plants were proposed as a species in 1990 by Hong Tao and with the name *P. ostii*. Both proposals were bizarre. The assumption that all the plants commercially cultivated, both overtly and covertly, for centuries must have had a wild ancestor is not unreasonable, but whether any truly wild plants have been found is uncertain. Also

Central Plains Mudan, reflecting the main area of development, now most strongly concentrated on Luoyang in Henan and Heze in Shandong. Various sub-groups such as the South-West cultivar group, are recognised, albeit overlapping and imprecisely delineated. The long history of these plants is understandably very erratically recorded despite their great importance in past and present Chinese culture, so various mysteries and uncertainties about their origins are only to be expected. In particular the ancestral species most prominently involved is unclear and the most likely species is now very uncommon. This is *P. jisha-nensis,* (called the choice of name seems perverse unless either largesse or a subtle sense of humour is involved. As it is all the plants grown in farms and gardens that once had the traditional and well-known (in China at least) name of Feng Dan Bai have suddenly become species *P. ostii* plants. They have apparently not been much used deliberately in the development of overtly ornamental hybrids. Pink flowered forms exist (Feng Dan Fen) and purplish-pink forms (Feng Dan Zi) and white with a purplish-pink centre. Some examples of Central Plains hybrids and of Gansu mudan have morphological features that seem clearly derived from Feng Dan peonies.

Gansu Group

The fourth group is Gansu Mudan, also sometimes referred to as the North-Western group. Here the crucial ancestral species is P. rockii in one form or another. There is evidence that Lanzhou, now a largely industrial city was in ancient times a centre of mudan production. It lies on the Silk Road so mudan are likely to have been taken to and from there. The appearance of some central Plains hybrids show some of the characteristics of Gansu Mudan. They have a dark area at the centre of the flower, a stain or smudge or flare if not the pronounced and striking blotch that is a distinctive characteristic feature of most Gansu Mudan. A few Central Plains hybrids are relatively tall and some have compound leaves quite like those of most Gansu Mudan and some are more hardy than others so the genetic influence of *P. rockii* or Gansu Mudan seems likely. The emergence of Gansu Mudan as a substantial and important group of cultivated hybrid peonies is a relatively recent phenomenon and is essentially due to Chen Dezhong's passion and inspiration. As such, although there are (or were) some ancient cultivars that can be assigned to this group, we can say with certainty that most of the earlier modern cultivars in this group are the result of deliberate crossings of true wild *P. rockii* (collected as simply Ziban Mudan, purple-blotched mudan) with central plains mudan. Subsequent cultivars use the earlier cultivars among the parent plants so we have the usual situation where the most recent additions are hybrids of hybrids of hybrids etc. The development of this group and the questions surrounding the various names attached, accurately or loosely, to plants in this group, notably

Paeonia `Feng Dan Bai´

A `wild´ form of P. `Feng Dan Bai´ found in Shennongjia.

P. rockii and Gansu Mudan but also *papaveracea*, *linyanshani* and *taibaishanica* are discussed in more detail in Chapters 3, 4 and 6.

Others

The fifth group has no botanical or morphological coherence. It is the remaining identified mudan taxa grouped together simply for convenience and to give them an appropriate perspective in mudan as a whole, in particular the apparent absence of significant influence by them in the major hybrid groups. There are two accepted and significant species, *P. szechuanica/decomposita* and *P. qiui*.

Small plants of *P. szechuanica/decomposita* with short, broad leaflets regarded as ssp. rotundifolia and on the left parts of leaves where the leaflets are intermediate.

P. szechuanica/decomposita. An example with narrow leaflets.

above and below: Baokang Mudan: plants found in the wild but presumably of cultivated origin.

Paeonia qiui

P. qiui type without wild provenance.

It is, in our view, greatly to be regretted that eminent Chinese botanists have mistakenly interpreted the rule of precedence in botanical nomenclature as obliging them to replace the fairly well established name *P. szechuanica* by the dreadful name *P. decomposita* coined by Handel-Mazzetti in 1939. Szechuan is the earlier Western spelling of Sichuan, the province where this species is mainly found. It has single pink flowers and is most notable for its complex leaves with very small individual leaflets. As far as we know it has not been used deliberately in the development of the cultivated hybrids but the small leaflets of some Gansu mudan suggest that it may possibly have been involved. Some examples with shorter, more rounded leaflets are designated ssp. *rotundifolia*. *P. qiui* seems to be less rare in the wild than was first believed, although many of the few plants in cultivation have the appearance of hybrids with the species as it has been described.

There are also several minor proposed species all of which have intermediate morphology between plants of the species or groups already mentioned. These include *P. yananensis*, *P. baokangensis* and *P. ridleyi*. There is at least one significant and apparently wild population of each of the first two but whether the plants 'discovered' are regarded as natural hybrids or intermediates or are cultivated escapes depends mostly on the point of view of the author concerned and unless further significant populations are discovered it hardly matters.

Basic references (see also Chapter 5) that will lead to many others:
Deyuan Hong and Kaiyu Pan (1999). A revision of the paeonia suffruticosa complex - Nordic Journal of Botany 19 (3) pp289 – 299.
Wu, Z., Raven, P. H. and Hong, D. Y. Hong (eds) (2001) Flora of China, Vol. 6 (Paeonaicae), Science Press, Beijing & Missouri Botanical Garden Press, St. Louis.
Zhao Xuan, Zhou Zhi-qin, Lin Qi-bin, Pan Kai-yu, Hong De-yuan (2004) Molecular evidence for the interspecific relationships in Paeonia sect. Moutan: PCR-RFLP and sequence analysis of glycerol-3-phosphateacyltransferase (GPAT) gene - Acta Phytotaxonomica Sinica 42 (3) 236-244.4
Xiangyun Zhu &Tau Hong (August 2005) Validation and neotypification of Paeonia rockii subsp. linyanshanii (Paeoniacae) - TAXON 54(3: 806-807
Wang Lianying et al (1997) Chinese Tree Peony, (English edition) China Forestry Publishing House.

3.   PAEONIA ROCKII

3.1   The evolution of the name

3.2   A compromise proposal

3.3   Observed Characteristics and Distribution of *Paeonia rockii*

3.4   Evidence from Molecular Analysis

3.1 The evolution of the name

It is crucial to bear in mind that in China the wild plants, mudan with purple-black blotched white flowers, have been familiar plants for centuries. There, the different forms of what are now called *P. rockii* and other basically similar plants, which may or may not be other species or hybrids introduced into the wild, are known collectively as Ziban Mudan and distinctions that may be made between individual examples are done so partly on the place of origin. The following summary of the emergence of the name *P. rockii* is a summary of the application of Western botanical nomenclature by first Western and latterly Chinese botanists.

Bear in mind also that the emergence or establishment of a species name in literature is not the same as the identification and classification of plants in the wild or in cultivation.

1804   **Andrews:** *P. suffruticosa.* The new species name given to a cultivated hybrid (without blotched petals, actually a Central Plains Mudan).

1807   **Andrews:** *P. papaveracea.* The new species name given to a cultivated hybrid (with blotched petals, actually a Gansu Mudan).

1890   **Pratt:** specimen, presumed wild, collected; no field notes. This important but unfortunately ambiguous specimen appears to be the earliest example known of wild collected (if it was) mudan, at least in a herbarium (Kew) in the West. Stern later accepts this specimen as an example of *P. suffruticosa* with 'leaflets deeply and incisely divided'. Some leaflets do have a small tooth. This specimen probably is an example of *P. rockii*, but may be a Feng Dan plant or a hybrid.

1914   **Farrer:** wild plants (of *P. rockii*) seen and described (extravagantly, but with inadequate botanical detail) and regarded/referred to as a form of *P. suffruticosa*.

1922   **Licent:** presumed wild specimen collected, apparently of *P. rockii* (but originally named *P. obovata*).

1925   **Rock:** sees plants in cultivation, unidentified and now unidentifiable but very likely examples of both Gansu Mudan and Central Plains Mudan. Seed from these plants, in two different locations, is not actually collected by Rock but is sent by him to the Arnold Arboretum and subsequently distributed.

1936   **Stern:** receives from Cleveland Morgan, Montreal a plant derived somehow, but probably indirectly, from Rock's seed, and which is an example of Gansu Mudan, not a wild species plant in any sense.

1946   **Stern:** in his famous monograph discusses 'forms of P. suffruticosa', makes some incorrect statements about Rock's seed and uses the expression 'Rock's peony', but not as a formal name.

1958   **Stern:** refers to his plant as *P. suffruticosa* 'Rock's variety'.

1971   **Reath:** lists grafted plants of *'P. suffruticosa* (Rock's)' propagated from material received (directly or indirectly) from Stern.

1988   **Li Jiajue:** in his book *Linxia Mudan* explains why the purple-blotched wild mudan should be separated from the suffruticosa complex but assumes, incorrectly but understandably, that the plant named *P. papaveracea* is an example.

1990   **Haw and Lauener:** propose the name *P. suffruticosa* ssp *rockii* for Stern's plant and for Farrer's herbarium specimen (and other herbarium specimens) erroneously assuming they are the same. The source of their leaf drawing of *P. suffruticosa* ssp *rockii*, with lobed leaflets, is not given but it is apparently of Stern's hybrid plant. Farrer's specimen is incomplete but on balance, and maybe with hindsight, has unlobed leaflets. Curiously they do not even mention Pratt's readily available specimen.

1992   **Hong Tao:** proposes *P. rockii* as a separate species, but describes the leaflets as lobed, presumably influenced by Haw and Lauener's error.

1994   **Hong Tao:** proposes *P. rockii* ssp *linyanshanii* as a new subspecies of *P. rockii* with unlobed leaflets.

1998   **Hong Deyuan:** reverses Hong Tao's formulation and names the form with unlobed leaflets P. rockii ssp rockii and the form with lobed leaflets *P. rockii* ssp *taibaishanica*, ostensibly correcting Haw and Lauener's error and Hong Tao's development from it.

2005   **Zhu Xiangyun and Hong Tao:** rummage in the nomenclatural entrails and introduce the unusual spectacle of a mysteriously missing herbarium specimen (holotype) in an attempt to resuscitate linyanshanii as a subspecies name.

This bare outline omits many other contributions from these and other authors. Almost all share three characteristics: a selective use, possibly inadvertent, of what evidence is available; fieldwork that is inadequate for the complexity of the reality or is superficial or nonexistent; an apparent desire to present a simple picture without the qualifications, uncertainties and caveats that are needed for an accurate picture. We might add an absence of sustained experience of growing the various plants involved in cultivation where continuous direct comparisons can be made free of environmental variation. So it must be said that Chen Dezhong, with his substantial knowledge and experience of wild plants could have usefully contributed more than generously helping researchers and visitors.

Wild *Paeonia rockii* flowers from various locations

Wen Xian

Wen Xian

Baokang

Shennongjia

Shennongjia

Shennongjia

Shennongjia

Shennongjia

Shennongjia

Xinglong

Tianshui

Tianshui

above and right: Hu Xiaoling and flowers of *linyanshanii* form of *P. rockii* at Phedar Nursery.

above, center and right: *P. rockii* fromTaibaishan: flower, leaf and fruit.

Left:
Small plant of
P. rockii in Tanshui
(E): note both blue-
green and yellow-
green leaves;
also strong new
growth and flower/
fruit despite the
adverse growing
conditions.

Right:
P. rockii in Tanshui
(E) showing new
shoot from the
base.

P. rockii in Taibaishan showing new shoot from the base.

Linyanshanii form of *P. rockii* (from Shennongjia, Hubei) growing at Phedar Nursery, in mid April.

As we have already emphasised, the overall situation for the classification of wild mudan is genuinely difficult. The remnant wild populations are widespread and not easy of access. That is why they have survived. That said it is disappointing that so often authors have indulged in the traditional shortcomings of botanical taxonomy when the obvious complexity demands much greater care. The herbarium specimens, of which too much is made, never have information about the size of the population they are taken from nor about its homogeneity and the extent to which the specimen is truly representative. This information may well be difficult to obtain but even comments pointing out its absence might induce some much needed caution. Some are from plants in cultivation. A striking feature of the herbarium sheets at Kew is the annotations by subsequent botanists about the name of the taxon involved. In many cases they seem to us correct, in some sense, but no reasons are ever given and in some cases the critical evidence cannot be discerned from the actual specimen, filament colour for example. The botanist making the annotation may never have seen a wild plant let alone have experience of the source population but nevertheless feels able to comment on a wild-collected specimen. This demonstrates a familiar trait, a punctilious regard for the minutiae of nomenclatural rules (absent from some places in this text) and much less regard for solid, consistent, interlocking botanical evidence. Careful study of much of Hong Deyuan's exten-

sive output when coupled with some experience of growing examples of the plants in question reveals superficiality and a lack of consistency. Arguments put forward in one context are not made elsewhere where they are equally valid. A particularly relevant example concerns plants with intermediate morphology. Lumping together all the very diverse plants of the *P. delavayi* complex because homogeneous populations have not been found and there is a continuous spectrum of flower colour and leaf and plant form is at least reasonable. But then the separation of two subspecies of *P. rockii* and of *P. decomposita/szechuanica* on the basis of differences in leaflet form when no evidence is given of population homogeneity and when intermediate leaf forms can be easily found seems perverse. Different criteria for species designation in different genera is unavoidable but within the same genus it begins to look like the taxonomy of Babel. Perhaps if less of Hong Deyuan's fieldwork had been done by his students and he was less determined to refute Hong Tao's work his own work on mudan taxonomy would be more consistent and more convincing. (Incidentally, other observers have reported seeing some homogeneous populations of *P. delavayi*.)

Wild P. rockii leaves from various locations with line drawings of leaves and herbarium sheets for comparison.

Wen Xian

Wen Xian

Hong Deyuan´s line drawing of *P. rockii ssp. rockii* leaf

Tanshui (E)

Tanshui (E)

Tanshui (E)

Taibaishan

Taibaishan

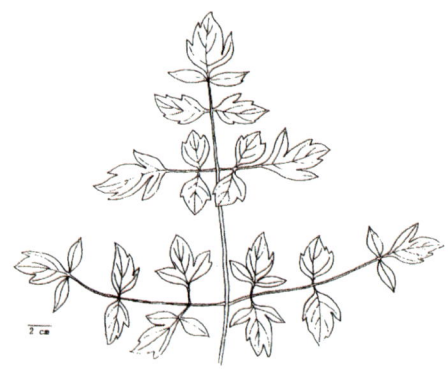

Hong Deyuan's line drawing of `*P. rockii ssp.taibaishanica*' leaf.

Baokang

A herbarium sheet at Kew of *P. rockii* from Baokang

The herbarium sheet at Kew of Pratt's specimen.

The herbarium sheet at Kew of Licent's specimen.

A herbarium sheet at Kew of G. P. Baker's plant.

Two of the herbarium sheets at Kew of Stern's plant at Highdown.

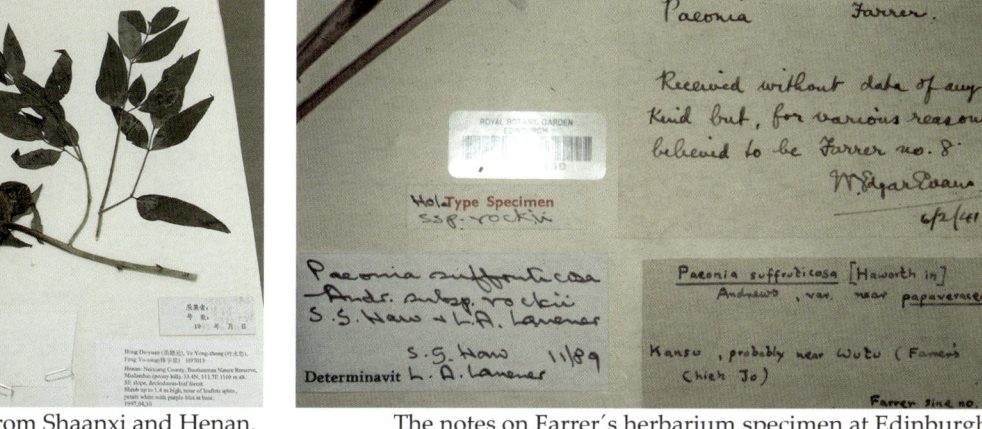

The herbarium specimen at Edinburgh assumed to have been collected by Farrer.

Two herbarium sheets at Kew of *P. rockii* from Shaanxi and Henan.

The notes on Farrer's herbarium specimen at Edinburgh.

Above: Four leaves of *P. szechuanica/decomposita* showing extreme and intermediate forms.

3.2 A compromise proposal about *Paeonia rockii*.
The present summary overview of ziban mudan growing in wild places: 'two subspecies of *P. rockii* based solely on different leaflet shape and all others regarded as hybrids in one sense or another' seems to us unsatisfactory because we know of wild populations where the leaflet shapes are neither one form nor the other. However it will probably be accepted for the foreseeable future until a concerted programme of much more thorough fieldwork and population analysis can be carried out coupled with equally thorough molecular analysis.

We suggest the following compromise proposal for the species *Paeonia rockii* as a helpful and more accurate representation of the reality, and which enables the main protagonists to depart with their 'honour' intact:
Paeonia rockii is defined and characterised below (and in the illustrations) but within the varied morphology two 'extreme' forms can be distinguished: *linyanshanii* as described by Hong Tao with all or almost all leaflets unlobed, and *taibaishanica* as described by Hong Deyuan with all or almost all leaflets significantly lobed.

3.3 Observed Characteristics and Distribution of *Paeonia rockii*

The description and comments that follow, and the pictures of herbarium and live true wild specimens, are not presented as a revision. They illustrate the comments above and in some cases add to what is 'well-known'. The description of *P. rockii* is based entirely on wild plants that we have seen. The locations and the allied comments are all and only based on first-hand experience. None are extracted from other publications so in that sense they are self-evidently an incomplete part of the whole picture.

Wild *P. rockii* plants have single flowers at the tips of branches/twigs with two, or very rarely three, whorls of petals. Normally there are 10 petals called, if necessary, primitive petals. Occasionally there are flowers with 11 or12 petals. The petals are thick, usually almost round or heart-shaped, sometimes fan-like, about 7-11cm long and 6-10cm wide. In cultivation and growing in 'better' conditions, the number of petals of the flower sometimes increases. Instinctively the question 'How frequently is sometimes?' arises and the best answer we can offer is 'Certainly not often enough to be expected but often enough not to be a great surprise'. A more precise answer needs many authentic plants from many locations and several years of testing and observation. The flower colour is white and at the base of the petals there are distinct but variably sized blotches, usually purple-black. The filaments and the stigma and the sheath are white or cream-white or very faintly green-white. These characteristics are critical. The sheath initially encloses or almost encloses the carpels and recedes as they develop. Leaves are bi-pinnate with 15 to 40, rarely up to 70 leaflets. Leaflets are mid- to dark green, possibly bluish green above, below they are grey-green with sparse fine hairs. Leaflets (collectively) vary from almost entirely lobed or toothed to entirely unlobed or entire. The plants can be over two metres tall.

This basic description needs significant qualification. The flowers may be pale pink in bud and open to white, but this, and the leaf colour, does vary with the environmental conditions. The filament and sheath colour is critical, but of course there are plenty of Gansu Mudan with white filaments and a white(ish) sheath. Leaf structure varies from leaf to leaf, with usually less developed leaves with fewer leaflets nearer the tip of the branch/twig. In many cases there are complex or ambiguous leaflets with the appearance of two or three simpler leaflets fused together. Leaves tend to be larger when growing conditions enable the plant to grow vigorously. In shady situations there may be fewer, larger individual leaflets. Shoots from the base, sometimes said to be absent in true *P. rockii*, do occur in wild plants, albeit not as prolifically as with some Gansu Mudan. In some areas Ziban Mudan with pale to dark pink or bluish-pink flowers have been found in apparently wild situations.

Wild Ziban Mudan (*Paeonia rockii*) are found in the mountain areas 1,000 to 2,800 metres above the sea level in the mid and western parts of China. There are traces of wild Ziban Mudan in regions such as Song County in Henan in the east, Qilian Mountaneous areas in the north-west (Lanzhou, Lintao and Linxia), woodlands in Shennongjia in the south and high mountain woodlands in Ganquan County, Yan'an in the north.

Diagrammatic map of China with place names mentioned indicated.

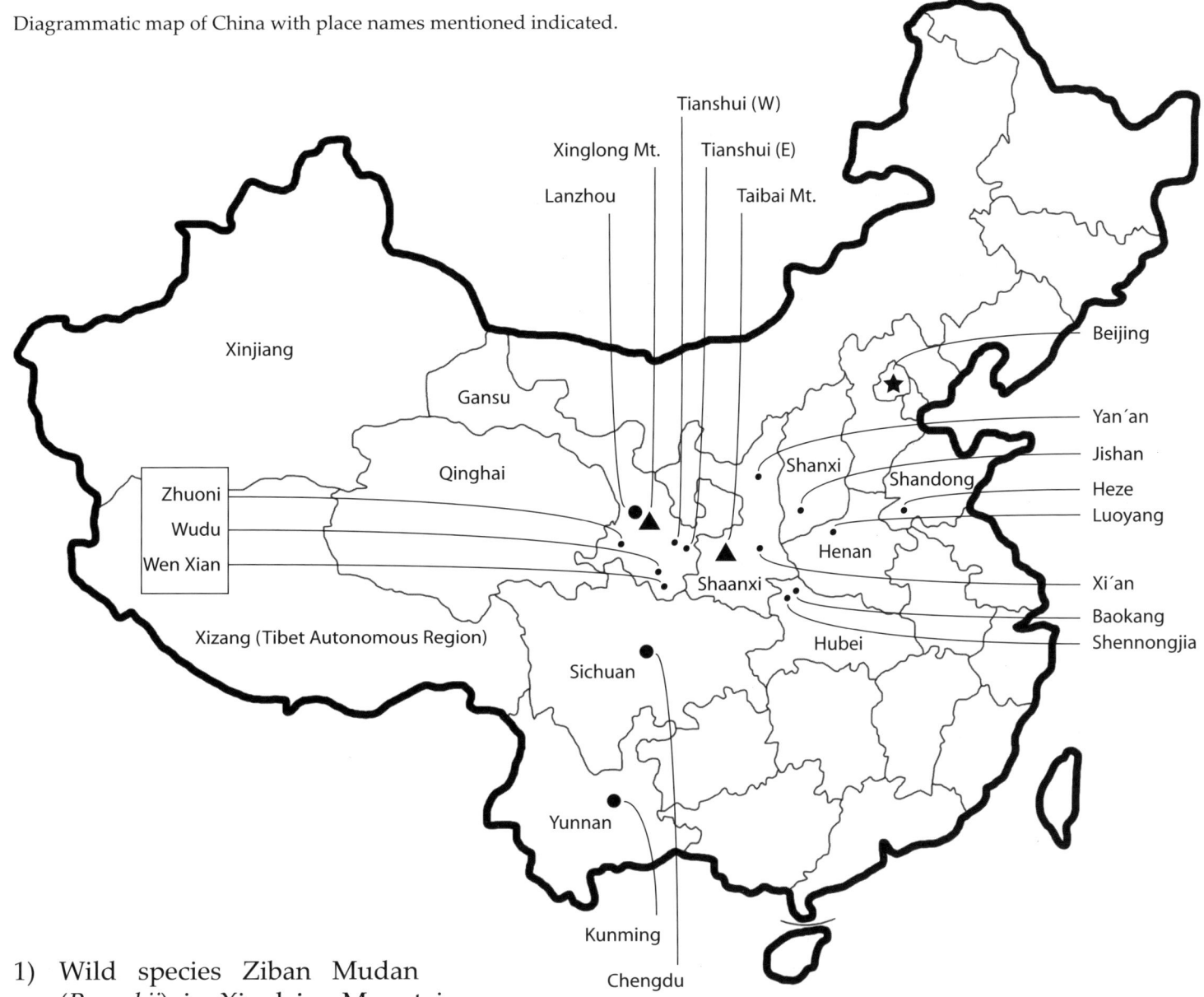

1) Wild species Ziban Mudan (*P. rockii*) in Xinglong Mountain (Maxian Mountain), Gansu: leaves have about 15 leaflets mostly well separated and unlobed, the underside of leaflets is noticeably hairy; white flowers. These *P. rockii* are one of the parents of the earlier 'modern' Gansu Mudan cultivars.

2) Wild species Ziban Mudan (*P. rockii*) in Wen Xian region, Gansu: leaflets variable, mostly about 25, unlobed, sometimes small and narrow. Leaves can, rarely, have as many as 70 leaflets; white flowers.

3) Wild Ziban Mudan in Yan´an region, Shaanxi: leaves have about 30 leaflets, mostly unlobed; flowers can be white or pink or reddish.

4) Wild species Ziban Mudan (*P. rockii*) in Shennongjia, including in Baokang, Hubei: leaves have mostly about 30 leaflets usually long and narrow, mostly unlobed, occasionally with small usually blunt lobes or teeth; white

flowers; flower sepals and bud are slightly big and thick. Other much more ambiguous plants are found in this region.

5) Wild species Ziban Mudan (*P. rockii*) in Tianshui in S. Gansu): leaves with up to thirty leaflets, mostly unlobed to variably mixed lobed and unlobed, white flowers.

6) Wild species Ziban Mudan (*P. rockii*) in Taibaishan, Shaanxi: leaves with mostly about twenty leaflets, mostly clearly lobed, white flowers.

In these summary descriptions 'white flowers' does not preclude flowers briefly pale pink on opening, and the number and form of leaflets is always complicated by leaflets, especially the terminal leaflet, which appear to be two or three simpler leaflets shortly fused at their base.

祁連濃霞

Paeonia Gansu Group 'Qi Lian Nong Xia'

4. MUDAN; GANSU MUDAN AND PAEONIA GANSU GROUP

4.1 On the term 'Mudan'

4.2 Historical Development of Gansu Mudan

4.3 Gansu Mudan: Current State of Propagation Horticultural Properties

4.4 Comparison of basic morphological features of plants of *P.rockii*, Gansu Mudan and Central Plains (suffruticosa) mudan

---

4.1 On the term `Mudan'; in particular on `MUDAN' and/or SHAOYAO and/or PAEONIA

We think there is no doubt that shaoyao means peonies or paeonia in general and herbaceous peonies in particular and mudan means woody peonies. However it is not a simple matter of translation because Chinese characters/prose can not be treated like words/prose of eg another European language, and in what might be called commercial literature nowadays the two words in pinyin are not always used carefully.

There is precise evidence in Professor Li Jiajue's 1988 and 1999 books (in Chinese) 'Linxia Mudan' and 'China Mudan and Shaoyao'. The first part of the main text of the latter is a careful review of references to peonies in ancient Chinese texts. His first sentence translates as 'Mudan and shaoyao are both plants of shaoyao belonging in shaoyao category/office'. In other words 'Mudan and shaoyao are sections of the genus shaoyao (paeonia) in family shaoyao (paeonaicea)'. Note that 'shaoyao belonging' is to be read as a single entity like 'shaoyao-belonging' not as 'shaoyao that belong to'.

In his evidence on the emergence and meaning of 'mudan' Li Jiajue refers to several ancient texts. A critically important one is the famous 'Compendium of Materia Medica' by Li Shizhen in the Ming Dynasty (1368 - 1664). In it he says Mudan was named because it "is mostly red.

It bears seed and produces shoots from its root. So it is referred to as Mu, the colour of the flowers is red so it is called Dan", Mu in this context meant 'it could be propagated with nutrient'.

Zheng Qiao in the Song Dynasty (960-1279) wrote in his 'Tong Zhi: Kun Chong Cao Mu Lue' (General Records: on Insects and Grasses (herbs) and Woody Plants) "What has been named woody shaoyao in olden times and today is mudan. As for mudan, its flowers are lovely like shaoyao, its root is woody, so it got its name as woody shaoyao. Mudan did not have a name at the beginning so it got its name from shaoyao."

Zheng Qiao quotes from 'Fu Lian Fa' (Methods of Making and Applying/Taking Medicine) by An Qisheng (Qin Dynasty 221-207 BC) who said "there are two varieties of shaoyao: one is jin shaoyao and the other is mu shaoyao. The jin shaoyao is white in colour and contain fat; the woody shaoyao is purple in colour and has a lot of veins. This can be confirmed by checking the roots." An Qisheng was from Langya (today's Linyi in Shandong Province).

Li Jiajue concludes that "It can be seen that during Qin and Han (206 BC - 220 AD) dynasties, the names, woody shaoyao and mudan, occurred almost simultaneously. This also shows that it has been more than 2000 years since our ancestors realised the medical significance of mudan."

A flower and leaves from the Gansu Mudan at Ness B.G. Cheshire.

The characters for shaoyao include 'pieces' of characters associated with medicine and grass (and spoon!). The current mu of mudan is a rare character with implications of earth/soil and propagation but when used with li, 'muli' means oyster. Part of the character implies male or ox. Dan is also a rare character, literally an archaic word for red (the usual, prosaic word is hong), but which is also used to mean 'of value' or 'special', rather like gold is used in English.

Li Jiajue, 1988. Linxia Mudan. Beijing: Science and Technology Publishing House. ISBN 5304-0371-0/S-26. (In Chinese)
Li, Jiajue, 1999. China Mudan and Shaoyao. Beijing: China Forestry Publishing House. ISBN 7-5038-2107-8. (In Chinese)

4.2 Historical Development of Gansu Mudan

Basic historical background

The Gansu Plain is one of the places traditionally and historically associated with the production of Mudan as ornamental plants. They have been cultivated there for more than one thousand years. Gansu Province is also one of the areas for growing the Chinese medicine danpi (the root bark of the tree peony) although in effect any region where Mudan grow (or once grew) in the wild is associated with danpi. Of the eighty-one

counties and cities in the province more than half grow Mudan with Lanzhou, Linxia, Lintao and Longxia as the centres of production both now and in the past.

There are references to peonies and peony growing in texts from about two thousand years ago and archaeological evidence from a thousand years earlier still. However it was in the two Han Dynasties (206-220), possibly earlier, that people started to pay serious attention to the medical use of Mudan and to appreciate the beauty of Mudan. When Emperor Yang of the Sui Dynasty (581-618) ordered the planting of Mudan in imperial gardens, varieties of Mudan were collected in Luoyang and became the earliest Central Plains group. In the Tang Dynasty that followed (618-907) politics, the economy and culture developed rapidly and people in the capital city of Changan became obsessed with Mudan. In the Northern Song Dynasty (920-1127) there was great progress in production skills and varieties began to be propagated by grafting. In the Ming Dynasty (1368-1644) there was another widespread surge of interest and development and the propagating centre moved to Haozhou (Haoxian City in Anhui Province today) and then on to Caozhou (Heze, Cao County in Shangdong Province today) and the capital city Beijing. The propagation of Mudan also developed in places like Lanzhou and Linxia in Gansu in the Northwest.

Lanzhou was called "Gold City" in the Qin and Han Dynasties and was an important city along the ancient Silk Road. Mudan would have been traded along the Silk Road with Gansu Mudan travelling eastwards and meeting Central Plains Mudan. According to the written record of "New Gansu Chronology" published near the end of the Qing Dynasty (1644-1911), Mudan were grown "in all the government buildings and the most popular ones were from Lanzhou with all sorts of colours". This showed that Lanzhou, the ancient Gold City, has been a centre of Mudan cultivation.

Chen Dezhong's extensive experimentation and breeding programme at Peace Peony Nursery has in a sense restored Lazhou's position. His development of new cultivars involved Central Plains varieties and true wild species plants now called *P. rockii*. It also involved the traditional varieties, or at least existing examples, of Gansu Mudan and effectively subsumed them in his extensive range of new cultivars.

Current state of propagation

The First Lanzhou Mudan Exhibition was held at Peace Peony Nursery in May 1991. The large plants and over 200 varieties of Gansu Mudan with their tall branches, abundant flowers, variety of colours and wonderful fragrance attracted a lot of attention. Subsequently Peace peony Nursery plants started to appear in various plant shows all over China and won many awards. They began to be propagated by other nurseries and to be exported abroad. This development has accelerated in recent years with growth of the Chinese economy so now they are widely available from many nurseries and dealers few, if any, of whom will ever acknowledge the original source of the plants. Peace Peony Nursery has already distributed about 150,000 named cultivars and unnamed seedlings, mostly in China.

Horticultural Qualities of Gansu mudan

Gansu Mudan have now been grown easily and successfully in many different environments. In China, in addition to Gansu, they have been thoroughly tested in Beijing, Shanghai, Inner Mongolia, Tibet, north-eastern provinces, Xingjiang and Hubei. During these tests plants experienced floods, drought and sandstorms and most coped well. These formal experiments have been mainly to establish their suitability for greening barren land in harsh conditions and selection continues to find particular varieties best suited to extreme situations. As ornamental plants in gardens and municipal planting they have grown well in many other areas. It is nicely ironic that while Gansu Mudan, at least the single, white form, remained one of the most sought after ornamental garden plants in western horticulture and were regarded as mysterious and almost mythical, they were being routinely tested in various harsh environments in China.

Established Central Plains (suffruticosa) hybrids in front and established Gansu Mudan behind at Peace Peony Nursery.

Although Gansu Mudan originate from a classic, moderately severe, continental climate in Gansu, exported plants have proved to be extremely adaptable and flourish equally well in Western, Mid-West and Eastern States of North America, and throughout Europe including Scandinavia and the Balkans. Their cultural requirements can be summarised as: reasonably nutritious soil that does not become waterlogged and an adequate water supply, particularly in Spring while they are becoming established. They will grow well in shade, within reason, and are undamaged by severe winters and hot summers. Persistent high humidity is far from ideal for them but in almost any situation they are worth trying.

4.4 Comparison of basic morphological features of plants of *P.rockii*, Gansu Mudan and Central Plains (*suffruticosa*) mudan growing at Peace Peony Nursery, Lanzhou, Gansu.

	Wild P.rockii from Xinglong Mts	Gansu Mudan/ Paeonia Gansu Group	Central Plains Mudan
form	overall tall and big	80% big, 12% medium, 8% small	relatively small and short
branches	long & thin	long & thick	short & thick
leaf	hairy, 15 leaflets (more in other locations)	80% hairy, 85 % with 15 (or more) leaflets, 15% with 9 leaflets	not hairy, 9 leaflets
leaflets	narrow & small, mostly unlobed	very varied, mostly lobed	round & big, lobed
bud	small & pointed	mostly rather round & big	round & big
flower type	single, 11 cm in diameter	flower head mostly upright; various types; over 11 cm in diameter	hanging; various types; over 11 cm in diameter
flower colour	white, often pink at first	many colours	many colours
blotch	black	colour and form varies greatly, often bleeding out a different colour	some plants have a dark basal blush
back blotches	occasionally, small & faint	large & strong in some cultivars	occasionally, faint
scent	strong	usually strong and pleasant	faint, usually pleasant
stamens	filaments white, normal anthers	varied colours and forms	varied colours & forms
carpels	5 carpels	0-13 carpels, usually 5	0-13 carpels, usually 5-9
stigmas	white	varied colours	varied colours
sheath	white	varied colours	usually brownish red
seed	small but many	varied quanitiy and size	mostly few
flowering period	about 15 days	about 24 days	about 25 days

For most characters it is possible to find specimens that are exceptions to these descriptions. When grown with Central Plains hybrids the flowering period of Gansu Mudan is usually about a week later.

5.   `ROCK'S PEONY'* – THE TRUE STORY
Will McLewin and Chris Sanders

A Long Preamble: the Myth, the Reality and an Explanation

The title of this chapter is deliberately perverse. The early twentieth century botanist, explorer and plant collector Joseph Rock **was** involved in the introduction of Gansu Mudan to Europe and North America. There **is** a true wild species peony now called *P. rockii* which commemorates his name but he in no sense discovered or introduced it nor ever saw a wild plant. There **are** plants in cultivation which have labels that involve his name but they do not constitute a clone or even a Group in the current formal sense and in most cases their provenance is uncertain to a greater or lesser degree.

In essence there is no such thing as 'Rock's peony', or rather there are many different plants labelled or referred to as 'Rock's peony', or 'Rock's variety' or Peony 'Joseph Rock', or Peony suffruticosa 'Joseph Rock ' or Peony suffruticosa 'Rock's form' or some other variation on these names. None of these are *Paeonia rockii* (unless by some extraordinary mischance). The different names do not necessarily refer to different and distinct plants or groups of plants and no one of these names, as used up to now, represents a particular clone. Exceptions to this, for example one individual propagating one plant vegetatively and labelling them with one of these names, does not preclude the same name being used elsewhere for different plants, nor does it preclude plants which could or should properly be given one of these names actually being labelled with an entirely different name. All are simply examples of Gansu Mudan with more-or-less white flowers, of which there are many more examples with Chinese names or no particular name at all. Aside from the many cultivars illustrated in Section Three which have originated in China, there are particular clones which have originated in Europe or North America for which the use of a clonal or cultivar name is appropriate. The two most important emerge from the details of the true story. Alternatively, all such plants with their various

---

*In the term 'Rock's peony' the single quotation marks are used ironically. As we have pointed out 'Rock's peony' is an ambiguous expression and within the Gansu Mudan context it is misleading and almost meaningless. This use of single quotation marks is entirely distinct from their recommended use for validly published cultivar names.

names could collectively be regarded as a cultivar group based on morphological characteristics, but there is little virtue in attaching a cultivar group name to a subset of Gansu Mudan on the basis of the historical accident of having been grown in the West and previous inappropriate nomenclature. In addition the impossibility of describing such a (sub)group in a useful and usable way is immediately apparent from the first few pages of pictures in Section Three.

Our use of 'true' is admittedly provocative. 'The truth' is an elusive entity that can only be sought, never found (with absolute certainty), particularly in contexts such as this one. However, as in this case we have sought it more diligently and with more success than others who have pronounced on the subject, we feel justified in using the word.

The myth

The story of the so-called discovery in China of 'Rock's Peony' by the American plant collector Joseph Rock has been told a number of times in books and magazines. A recent version, similar to many others, is as follows: "He [Rock] was at the Zhoni (sic) lamasery, a Buddhist monastery in Gansu Province, for the winter of 1925-26 and saw the wonderful peony growing in the lamasery garden. He photographed the plant and collected its seeds, later distributing them to botanical gardens on both sides of the Atlantic. .... A fine specimen of *P. rockii* grown from Joseph Rock's original seed is still there [in Frederick Stern's garden at Highdown in Sussex]".

Leaving aside the obvious question of what Rock could have seen of a wonderful peony in winter most of this account is wrong. In particular, the fine specimen at Highdown is not *P. rockii*.

The Reality

The basic outline of the true story of 'Rock's peony' is that Rock sent three separate batches of shrubby peony seed to Charles Sargent at the Arnold Arboretum (plus another batch, described by Rock as shrubby peony seed but actually herbaceous peony seed and not relevant to this story, but see below). These were almost certainly collected for him in his absence from shrubby peonies in cultivation in two separate locations. Some of these seeds were then sent to certain botanic gardens and to certain individuals, not including Stern. Some recipients germinated some seeds and subsequently seeds and small plants were distributed. Ten years after the initial distribution of the seed sent by Rock, Stern received a plant (very probably but not certainly the now famous one at Highdown) from Cleveland Morgan in Canada and subsequently exhibited flowers and distributed propagating material, seedlings and seed. There is no evidence to suggest that any of the many plants involved are other than cultivated hybrids, Gansu Mudan in fact, and all examples known to us are clearly Gansu Mudan and not *P. rockii*.

This outline indicates that in addition to Rock and Stern there are two other leading participants, Sargent and Morgan. They are almost never mentioned in other accounts but their involvement is crucially important. Our account of the historical section of the story is divided into four successive chronological periods which although they overlap and interact, mainly cover successive horticultural considerations. In each one of these four parts one of the major participants is prominent, and we give some brief biographical details there, although all are mentioned in other places. In addition to these four 'important' people whose documents are saved in archives and who are written about in articles and historical accounts and who, in fact, between them left the basis of all the subsequent misunderstanding, there are some other 'unimportant' people. They appear briefly in the account but their small items of evidence, preserved by chance, are crucial to uncovering the true story.

Before beginning our detailed account of the history of 'Rock's peony' we emphasise that comments like 'there is no evidence for' are, of course, to be read as 'we have found no evidence for', but also that where statements we regard as inaccurate have been made, and in most cases frequently repeated, no evidence has been given that adequately supports them.

An Explanation

As to why misinformation about a group of plants should have become so widespread, the simple answer is that overall the situation is genuinely complicated as explained in other chapters of this section, and everyone involved has been less than careful. The first mudan to be seen in the West were hybrids, the products of centuries of cultivation, but were named and described incorrectly as if they were true species plants (*P. papaveracea*, which is a Gansu Mudan, and *P. suffruticosa* and subsequent similar examples, which are Central Plains hybrids.) Farrer is sometimes credited with discovering *P. rockii*, in 1914 which is absurd. The plant had been well known to Chinese horticulturists for hundreds of years and evidently involved in hybridisation. But aside from this botanical imperialism, on finding *P. rockii* in the wild Farrer apparently did not make careful and detailed field notes to describe the plants. Instead, in 1914 in *The Gardeners Chronicle* and in 1917 in *On the Eaves of the World* he produced the two much quoted versions describing, as Stern puts it, "in his own characteristic way" his act of discovery and his emotions at the time. ("Through the foaming shallows of the copse I plunged........that single enormous blossom, waved and crimped into the boldest grace of line, of absolutely pure white.......the boss of golden fluff at the flower's heart......" and so on.) Farrer did collect at least one example of the flower and some leaf material, presumably intended for a herbarium specimen sheet. Unfortunately this specimen (and others of herbaceous peonies) was received from Mrs Farrer at Edinburgh only after a considerable lapse of time. It was identified (as *P. suffruticosa*) in 1941 by William Stearn who was working at the time on Stern's seminal and still important 1946 monograph *A Study of the Genus Paeonia* where, curiously, it is said that "unfortunately he [Farrer] did not collect specimens".

Most authors appear to have based their versions of the story directly or indirectly on Stern's account in his monograph and on very little else. Stern's information was, in turn, mostly derived from a letter he received from Rock in 1938 much of which is quoted in his monograph.

It is reproduced in its entirety here because what is not said is as significant as what is said. Rock recounts how he collected seeds from plants growing in the courtyard garden of the Yamen (official residence) of the lamasery of Choni (correct modern pinyin spelling Zhouni) in SW Gansu which he says he "occupied... for about a year". (In fact, for almost two years, he used it as a base from which to explore the surrounding area.) No date is given for the collection in the letter, although Rock does mention that the lamasery was "entirely destroyed and the lamas all killed in 1928 by the Mohammedans, so the plant (sic) does in all probability not exist any more as the entire Lamasery was burned to the ground". It is rather curious therefore that Stern should have stated in his monograph that "some time after 1932 [Rock] sent seed of a tree-paeony to the USA", although by the time he published *A Chalk Garden* in 1960 he had revised this to 1926 (closer, but still incorrect). However, this is just another of the errors, ambiguities and half-truths attributable to both Stern and Rock, which subsequent authors have uncritically repeated. To be fair to Stern, he did his best to find out about his own plant, but without complete herbarium specimens of wild plants and without first hand knowledge of the Chinese context and hampered by the passage of time and the 1939-45 war he failed to realise his plant was a cultivated hybrid. Stern's mistake was repeated, much less excusably, in 1990 by Haw and Lauener. They proposed a subspecies, ssp *rockii*, of *P. suffruticosa* that included Stern's plant, but without fieldwork or ever having grown or even seen true wild plants and partly on the basis of Farrer's very poor herbarium specimen. It should not be surprising that their detailed description of ssp. *rockii* also is erroneous in that while it fits Stern's hybrid it does not fit true wild *P. rockii*. Stern's main problem was the dearth of information concerning the collection and dispatch of the seed from Zhuoni, its arrival at the Arnold Arboretum and its subsequent distribution to other interested parties. Some twelve years were to elapse between the original receipt of the seed at the Arnold by Sargent and Stern's first sight, in 1938, of flowers similar to those that had made such an impression on Farrer 25 years before. Only then was Stern galvanised into trying to trace the details of the origin of his plant. Enquiries to the Arnold Arboretum no doubt received the same reply then as we have today – there are no records of any tree peony seed received from Rock. This even though meticulous records of every other wild collection he made, together with his field notes were and are available. To be fair to Rock, he was exceptionally resourceful and the only person of all those involved thoroughly familiar with Chinese culture and language, but he was apparently not interested in peonies. He was probably familiar with large-flowered mudan in cultivation in China and attached no great importance to the mudan seed he sent to Sargent. Indeed we guess that after its dispatch it had never crossed his mind until Stern's letter arrived.

So, although both Rock and Stern, subsequent to events, wrote clearly inaccurate comments which have certainly helped to create the misconceptions about 'Rock's peony', they carry no more blame than the many commentators since who, with one or two notable exceptions, have seemed determined to demonstrate the truth of Roy (Lord) Jenkins' observation that "meticulous research is almost always the enemy of good anecdote". Most bizarrely of all perhaps, Rock himself in 1953 presented RBG Kew with a specimen of 'Rock's peony', which is nothing of the kind, and not even a Gansu Mudan.

Fortunately, we have discovered enough evidence from other sources, notably Rock's original diaries at RBG Edinburgh, previously unpublished correspondence between Rock and his sponsors now available on the Arnold Arboretum web-site, Stern's papers at RBG Kew as well as the accession records in the archives of both Kew and Edinburgh, to be able to piece together **most** of the story of the introduction of Gansu Mudan into western gardens.

Part 1: Rock's Expedition to Gansu and the Background to It
Dr Joseph Francis Charles Rock (1884 -1962)

Josef Franz Karl Rock was born in 1884 in Vienna, Austria. He appears to have had an extraordinary linguistic ability and, according to the obituary by A. K. Chock, had by the age of sixteen mastered a number of foreign languages including Arabic, Chinese and Latin. In 1905, a year after graduating from Vienna University, he emigrated to the United States. As a young man Rock suffered from tuberculosis and presumably as a consequence went to Hawaii in 1907. (Hawaii had been annexed by the United States in 1899.) He regained his health there and in 1913 became a naturalized US citizen and anglicized his name to Joseph Francis Charles Rock. During this stage of his career he thoroughly explored the islands and developed a comprehensive herbarium of the native flora and published a number of authoritative books and scientific papers (in his adopted language, English). To his friends and colleagues there he was known as *Pohaku*, the Hawaiian word for rock. Before being appointed Professor of Systematic Botany at the College of Hawaii in 1919 he undertook plant introduction journeys to Malaysia in 1916 and 1919 and to Southern California in 1917 and a round the world trip in 1913/14.

With a secure reputation as a scientific botanist and plant explorer Rock finally left Hawaii in 1920. He was to spend the next three decades in active research and exploration in Asia. During this period he introduced literally thousands of Asiatic plants (including 439 species of *Rhododendron* alone) to the United States and gathered many more thousands of botanical, ornithological and zoological specimens, as well as taking over forty thousand photographs and mapping previously unknown regions. Numerous plants, birds and mammals commemorate his name. From his base in Li-chiang/Lijiang in the Chinese province of Yunnan he made a comprehensive study of the Naxi people, translated some of their literature and later published a dictionary of their language.

Rock is a truly heroic figure yet is not as well known, at least in the UK, as some of the other plant hunters of the first half of the twentieth century. There is no doubt that he was their equal in many respects and clearly superior in others.

The Arnold Arboretum Expedition to Kansu/Gansu

Note: for Chinese place names we use the modern pinyin transliteration, but in some places where the text is essentially quoting from historical accounts we use the spelling there followed by the modern spelling e.g. Kansu/Gansu. However the question of spelling place names in the latin alphabet is complicated when the local population is not Han Chinese but one of the many semi-autonomous ethnic minorities, who may well use their own transliteration scheme distinct from pinyin. Zhuoni (see below) is one place where this complication arises. Rock spelt it Choni; the pinyin spelling is Zhuoni; the indigenous (Naxi) transliteration is Jonê.

During the early years of his travels in Yunnan and neighbouring parts of Burma, Siam and Indo-China, Rock's chief sponsors were the US Department of Agriculture and the National Geographic Society. In the summer of 1924, he returned to Washington D.C. and visited the elderly Professor Sargent, Director of the Arnold Arboretum at Jamaica Plain, Boston, Massachusetts. Sargent had previously employed the by then famous English plant collector Ernest ("Chinese") Wilson to collect seeds of woody plants for the arboretum, mainly in the more southerly provinces of Hupeh/Hubei, Szechuan/Sichuan and Yunnan. Many of these introductions did not prove hardy enough to withstand the cold Massachusetts winters, so Sargent was keen to find tougher species or forms from the mountain ranges farther north. Wilson, who had suffered a nasty injury whilst returning down the Min Gorge in Sichuan after collecting thousands of bulbs of *Lilium regale* in September 1911, had long since retired from active exploration and was now working at the Arnold. Sargent saw that Rock was the ideal person to undertake an expedition to the Amne Machin/Animaqing/A'nyê Maqên Shan and Datong Shan ranges on the borders of Gansu and Tibet (both are now included in the province

of Qinghai). The Arnold Arboretum expedition, to be sponsored by Harvard University, was to take three years and Rock (salary $500 per month and a similar amount for expenses) immediately began to purchase essential equipment and instruments prior to setting sail from San Francisco bound for Shanghai in the first week of October 1924.

Rock arrived at Yunnanfu/Kunming, the capital city of Yunnan, essentially the starting point of the expedition, in early November 1924. This was an unsettled period in Chinese history and fighting and brigandage were rife in the province. It was December 13th when Rock and his caravan of twenty-six mules, porters, trained Naxi staff and heavy military escort set out on their long journey north.

The four-month danger-ridden journey initially followed the ancient caravan route via Chaotung/Zhaotong and Suifu/Shuifu to Chengtu/Chengdu. Rock had to delay there for a month until the route became safe to continue on via Mienchow/Mianyang and across the Gansu border to Kaichou/Wudu, Minchou/Min Xian and Choni/Zhuoni. The details are recorded faithfully in Rock's copious diaries and also in the numerous letters he wrote to Sargent and others at the Arnold. Only someone of his stubborn determination, tenacity and bravery would have contemplated let alone successfully accomplished such a venture. He and his caravan eventually reached Zhuoni on April 21st 1925. Zhuoni, then a village of some four hundred families and roughly 2000 inhabitants, according to Rock, lies in the valley of the Tao He, a tributary of the great Huang He (Yellow River), at an altitude of 2500 metres. It was the centre of a semi-independent Tibetan principality of the same name which was ruled over by a hereditary prince called Yang Chi-ching. Rock described it thus: "The village is by far the best situated spot in Kansu Province, and the Prince's territory, which I traversed from north to south and east to west, is the choicest bit of land. Nowhere else in Kansu are there such forests, and the scenery is unsurpassed". Prince Yang (his actual title in the local Naxi dialect was *t'ssu* – chief or headman, *tusi* in pinyin) was in his mid thirties and was a cruel and rapacious leader by all accounts who treated his subjects abominably (he was later horribly murdered by his own

The photograph of the garden at the lamasery with peonies, mostly herbaceous, in flower.

surrounding mountains and valleys. He spent the next two winters there, writing up his field notes and sorting, labelling, packing and then dispatching specimens and the collected seed to Sargent at the Arnold Arboretum. He left Zhuoni for what was to be the last time on March 10th 1927.

(The articles by Rock published in the *National Geographical Magazine* and S. B. Sutton's book *In China's Border Provinces* among the references at the end of this chapter provide more details about the expedition. Rock's diaries are particularly recmended.)

people after Rock had left), but he nevertheless proved a good friend to Rock, helping him with letters of introduction, procuring supplies and pack animals and even lending him money. As he was also the Grand Lama of the nearby lamasery he was able to provide Rock with comfortable accommodation there. The lamasery was situated on a plateau about five hundred feet above and slightly to the west of the village. It was said to be the third largest of its kind and was almost a village in itself, with 172 buildings plus a further ten large and small chanting halls within its walls. Around 700 "malodorous" monks were in residence at the time, although more had been present in earlier years. The Prince and his family resided in his own palatial yamen down in the village itself.

Rock had anticipated being well clear of the troubles affecting Yunnan and Sichuan, but found that fighting between the Mohammedans and the local Tibetans and hostile tribes such as the Tebbus and the Ngoloks, severely hampered his plans to get to the mountain ranges he had come to explore. (The province of Tibet at that time included much territory that is now included in the modern provinces of Qinghai, Gansu and Sichuan.) Rock, therefore, decided to make Zhuoni his base for the remainder of the expedition, returning there at the end of each foray into the

Part 2: The Peony Seed Sent by Rock and its Distribution
Professor Charles Sprague Sargent (1845-1927)

Unjustified assumptions about the mudan seed that Rock sent, or rather unquestioning acceptance coupled with fanciful extrapolation from Rock's letter to Stern, are a major reason for misconceptions about 'Rock's Peony', so it is important to examine what is known about the seed and where it came from.

The Lamasery Courtyard Garden and its Peonies
In his letter to Stern dated 30th August 1938 Rock states that "The seed of the Paeonia about which you enquire I collected from plants which grew in the Yamen of the Choni Lamasery…". Rather confusingly also he refers to "the plant" and several times to "it" as if there was only one plant, at least of this particular kind. On the other hand he says that "There were no double-flowered ones, all were single", without making it clear whether they were all the same type. Further evidence of the presence of peonies there occurs in one of Rock's articles for the *National Geographic* – "Life Among The Lamas Of Choni", in which he refers to "a tiny courtyard filled with choice peonies, lilacs and other flowers".

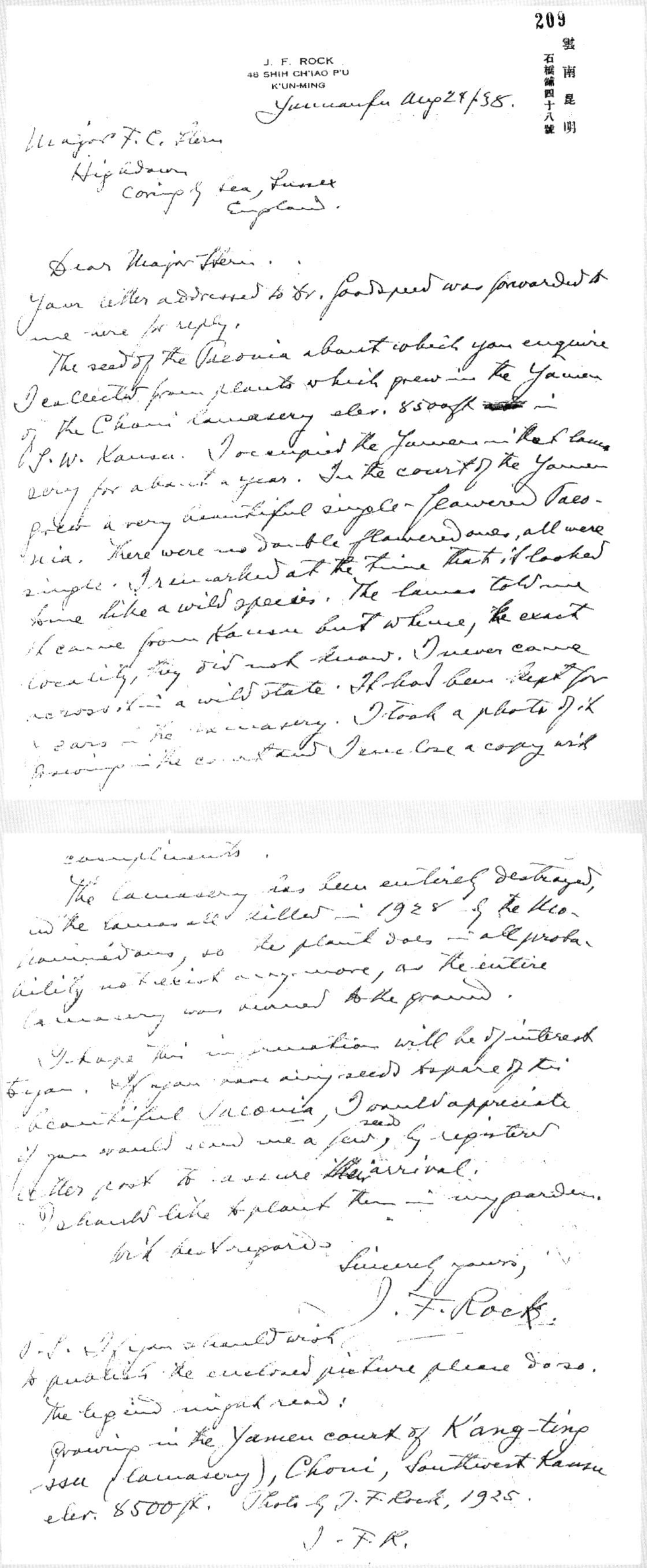

J. F. ROCK
48 SHIH CH'IAO P'U
K'UN-MING
Yunnanfu Aug 24/38

Major F.C.Stern
 Highdown
  Goring by Sea, Sussex
   England.

 Dear Major Stern,
Your letter addressed to Dr. Godspeed was forwarded
 to me here for reply.
 The seed of the Paeonia about which you enquire
I collected from plants which grew in the Yamen
of the Choni lamasery elev. 8500 ft in
S.W. Kansu. I occupied the Yamen in that lama
sery for about a year. In the court of the Yamen
grew a very beautiful single-flowered Paeonia. There were no double flowered ones, all were
single. I remarked at the time that it looked
to me like a wild species. The lamas told me
it came from Kansu but whence, the exact
locality, they did not know. I never came
across it in a wild state. It had been kept for
years in the lamasery. I took a photo of it
growing in the court and I enclose a copy with

compliments.
 The lamasery has been entirely destroyed,
and the lamas all killed in 1928 by the Mo-
hammadans, so the plant does in all probability not exist any more, as the entire
lamasery was burned to the ground.
 I hope this information will be of interest
to you. If you have any seed to spare of this
beautiful Paeonia, I would appreciate
if you could send me a few seed, by registered
letter post to assure their arrival.
 I should like to plant them in my garden.
  With best regards
          Sincerely yours,
           J. F. Rock.
P.S. If you should wish
to publish the enclosed picture please do so.
 The legend might read:
 Growing in the Yamen court of K'ang-ting
 ssu (lamasery), Choni, Southwest Kansu
 elev. 8500 ft. Photo by J.F.Rock, 1925.
          J. F. R.

Rock's letter to Stern

娇
妹

Paeonia Gansu Group 'Jiao Mei'

The photograph that accompanied the letter was subsequently used by Stern to illustrate an article entitled "The Moutan Paeony" in the *Journal of the Royal Horticultural Society* for December, 1939. It shows the whole garden, which appears to be no more than perhaps 60 square metres. According to Rock's diary, it is likely that this photograph was taken on May 18th 1925. It is not possible to make out much detail, but most of the plants do look like peonies, some of which are in flower. However, there appears to be one plant only, which by its shape and stature and the poise of its flowers could be a Gansu Mudan or *P. rockii* tree peony. It is not clear whether the other plants are mudan or herbaceous kinds. The photograph is missing from Stern's file at Kew, but the original print, reproduced here, is held at Edinburgh (along with 20,000 others).

The question of the number and kind of plants from which the seed was collected and whether other different mudan were also present is critical. It has an important bearing on whether the plant or plants could have been true *P. rockii* to start with and whether the seed could have been true *P. rockii* seed. Rock gave his opinion of the plant in the letter to Stern: "I remarked at the time that it looked to me like a wild species. The lamas told me it came from Kansu, but whence, the exact locality, they did not know. I never came across it in a wild state. It had been kept for years in the Lamasery". Stern twice embellished this: in a note in the *Journal of the Royal Horticultural Society* in 1959 he wrote "The Lamas told him that it came from the mountains of Kansu, known as "Min Shan", which DR. ROCK tells me are limestone" and in *The Chalk Garden* (1960) "The lamas told him that it came from the mountains of that district [SW Kansu]". Stern and others, including Haw and Lauener who described and named *P. rockii* (as *P. suffruticosa* ssp *rockii*) for the first time in 1990, seem to have accepted without question that plants in cultivation raised from the original seeds sent back by Rock belong to the wild species. It is conceivable that the original plant(s) in the lamasery were transplanted there from a wild source and could, therefore, have been true *P. rockii*. It is conceivable that if there was more than one actual plant all were true *P. rockii*. It is conceivable that there were no other kinds of tree peony present either in the same small garden or any other gardens nearby in the lamasery complex for cross pollination. Our view is that other possibilities are much more plausible. There is substantial evidence, at least from plants in cultivation, that isolated plants (or more than one clonal plant together) are self sterile. If this is the case and if there was only the one mudan in the garden, as appears likely from the photograph, then some other mudan must have been present nearby to pollinate it. So even if the plant in the picture was actually true *P. rockii* any seed collected from it is likely to have been hybrid seed. And in spite of what Rock said in his letter it is by no means certain that any of the few plants that were grown from his seed actually came from seed of the mudan in the lamasery garden (see below). What is much more likely to have been the case in our opinion is that the plant(s) were of hybrid origin to start with. Bear in mind that mudan had been cultivated and hybridised in China for centuries and these included Ziban Mudan (literally purple-blotched mudan) in Gansu, and that such plants were not uncommonly planted near temples and monasteries. Rock's comment that "it looked to me like a wild species" is in our view not significant. He would surely have come across Central Plains hybrids in cultivation in China which would mostly if not all have been doubles so the phrase "like a wild species" means, in our view, nothing more than the flowers were single. Incidentally, it is curious that Rock nowhere refers to the blotches on the petals that are a prominent and characteristic feature of Gansu Mudan and *P. rockii* but not of other peonies.

The Prince's Garden

In all the accounts of 'Rock's peony' that we have read, no one has ever referred to the garden of the Prince of Zhuoni or the role that the peonies there might have played in the story of 'Rock's peony'. Other than as an addendum to his field notes of wild plants (we presume), the only mention by Rock himself that we have found was in a letter to Sargent dated December 13th 1925. Right at the end of a long account of the seeds collected that autumn he casually remarked "I have also seeds of several Paeonia grown by the Prince of Zhuoni. These are tall plants and he says they come true to seed".

Rock's field notes for the various seed collections received at Kew and Edinburgh are preserved in the accession records at both places. They are typed, presumably from his handwritten originals. Three separate notes that refer to the mudan seed appear at the very end of the list and, in contrast to all the rest, do not have collection numbers. Rock's notes for these items read:

(1) "Paeonia sp. Shrub 4-5 ft tall, fls. very large, white. Grown in the garden of the Choni prince's Yamen, Choni. elev. 8500 ft. October 1925"

(2) "Paeonia sp. Shrub 3-4 ft. in the Lamaserie garden of Choni. -- large, colour ? October 1925"

(3) "Paeonia sp. Shrub 4-5 ft. fls. very large red, grown in the Choni Prince's Yamen. 8500 ft. October 1925"

As is evident, collections (1) and (3) refer to the Prince's garden in Zhouni itself, while collection (2) is from the courtyard garden in the lamasery 500 ft. above the village. In spite of the omission in the description of the latter, which we guess is due to the inability of the typist to decipher Rock's handwriting, this seed is presumably the subject of Rock's comments in his letter to Stern referred to earlier. The " elev. 8500 ft." for Zhouni is presumably simply an error, since Rock, in his letter to Stern, says that the lamasery also was at this height. (Estimations of altitude were not Rock's strong point – he once claimed that one of the peaks in the Amne Machin Range rivalled Everest.) The significance of the two collections from the Prince's garden increases later on when we discuss the plants known to have resulted directly from the seed sent by Rock (which do not include Stern's famous plant at Highdown).

There is another crucial point that should be highlighted here. In his letter to Stern, Rock stated that he collected the seeds from the plant (or plants) in the lamasery garden. The collection date given in the notes for all three of the tree peonies was simply "October 1925". However, Rock's diary clearly shows that he was away from Zhuoni from August 13th until December 3rd, so it is highly unlikely that he, Rock, could

have collected any of the seeds personally. This may not be of great significance, since Rock used a number of trained Naxi collectors, but by using the phrase "Rock collected seed [of the peony]" with its added veracity other authors appear to have misled themselves as well as their readers. It also begs the question of how Rock, on receipt of Stern's enquiry about the origin of the seed, could have known which plant(s) it had come from. (Quite apart from Stern's dubious assumption that his plant had come directly from the peony seed that Rock had sent.)

Incidentally, it is usually assumed that Rock, in his letter, was replying to an enquiry directly from Stern. In fact Stern had written to Professor Goodspeed at the University of California, the sponsors of Rock's 1932 expedition (to Western China and Tibet) believing that Rock had collected the mudan seed on that expedition. Stern's letter was forwarded from there to Rock in Kunming.

There was one other packet of peony seed in Rock's 1925 consignment. This was from plants in the wild (Tao river basin, 9000ft) and had the collectors number 13593. The plant was described as 1 to 2 feet high with flowers large, white, pink, red, and although Rock listed it as a shrubby peony it was later identified by Rheder and Kobuski as an example of the variable and widespread species P. anomala.

Rock recorded in his diary that he completed the labelling of seeds harvested that autumn together with corresponding herbarium specimens and despatched them to the Arnold Arboretum on December 15th 1925 (not in 1926 as reported by Stern in 'The Chalk Garden'). The mudan seeds were sent at the same time, but as far as is known unfortunately without any specimens, dried or otherwise, of the plants.

Arrival and Departure of the Mudan Seed

Rock's seeds, including the mudan seed, arrived at the Arnold Arboretum on the 12th February 1926. They must have been dealt with very promptly, because a letter addressed to the Director of Kew B.G. dated the 19th of that month and signed by Charles Sargent, advising of the dispatch of 151 packets of Rock's seeds, was date stamped at Kew on the 28th. The same letter was sent to Edinburgh, the only difference being that they were sent 148 packets. Presumably all the other recipients were treated similarly. Enclosed with each letter was a typed copy of Rock's field notes and a handwritten check-list with details of the collection numbers of all the seeds in that consignment. All that is, except for the mudan seeds, which had no numbers and were added on at the end. In fact, the Arnold does have the international distribution records of this and other Rock seed consignments, together with the total number of packets sent to each recipient, but not the details of exactly which seeds were sent where, so it is not possible to tell from the Arnold list who received some of the mudan seed. Stern, in his monograph, rather strangely we think, included a rather vague list which he and others have repeated in subsequent accounts. Strange, because we know he was in possession of a more extensive and more precise list at the time. The evidence for this is contained in a copy of a letter sent to him from Montreal by someone who was one of the original recipients of the seed. This was F. Cleveland Morgan, another major player in the story but one who has remained unmentioned in other accounts. Stern must have contacted Morgan early in 1938 seeking information as to who else might have received some of the original seed. Morgan, in turn, wrote to the Arnold and received two letters in reply dated 5th and 6th May 1938 from William H. Judd which he sent on to Stern. Judd worked at the Arnold for thirty years from 1920 to 1950, for at least part of that time as propagator and is commemorated in *Prunus* x *juddii* and *Viburnum* x *juddii.* These two letters are among the most crucial bits of evidence. In the first letter he mentions that Charles Sander, who was Sargent's gardener, had raised two plants "from the same lot of seed as yours" and that they had flowered in Sargent's garden. He also wrote that the colour of the petals was "pale lilac" and that there were two sheets from these two plants in the herbarium. In this letter he said that he did not know of anyone else who had received seed, but the very next day he wrote again to say that he had found others who had also been sent seeds.

The list given in the second letter was:

Royal Botanic Gardens Kew, UK
Royal Botanic Gardens Edinburgh, UK
Berlin-Dahlem Botanic Garden, Germany
Bergianska Botanical Garden Stockholm, Sweden
Professor A. P. Saunders, Clinton, New York
T. A. Havemeyer of Long Island, New York
Lionel de Rothschild, Exbury, UK
F. Cleveland Morgan, Montreal, Canada
Professor C. S. Sargent

This is not the complete list of recipients of seed from Rock's December 15th 1925 consignment. According to the Arnold's international distribution records botanic gardens or similar institutes in Nanjing, Hokkaido, Paris, Illinois, Leningrad and Ottawa also received seeds. Judd, in his letter, does not say how he found his list of recipients twelve years after the event so we can only guess whether it contains everyone to whom Sargent sent or intended to send the mudan seed. In fact there was at least one other recipient, namely Kenneth McDouall of Logan, Scotland.

An interesting question concerns whether Rock and all the recipients of the peony seed were aware of Farrer's account. It seems certain that Rock was not. He makes no suggestion in his diaries that he attached any great significance either to the packets of peony seed he sent or to the plants themselves. There is no evidence that any of the recipients of the seed, with the likely exceptions of Sargent and Saunders, made the connection or that the seed was regarded with any special attention.

The absence of a record at the Arnold of the three packets of mudan seed, and hence the role of Sargent in this part of the story had puzzled others before it puzzled us. It perplexed Stern for years, even up to 1967 when he died, aged 82. There is a letter amongst his papers at Kew dated in that year that shows it still troubled him then. In that letter, replying to an enquiry from one Leo J. Armatys, Stern refers to the Judd letters and

Paeonia Gansu Group 'Lan He'

蓝荷

bizarrely includes himself among the recipients of the seed. (Equally bizarre is Stern omitting, we assume, to examine the acquisition records at Kew, which would at least, as it did with us, have given him a basically correct chronology.) In fact Judd's first letter contains the vital piece of information that provided an explanation of the mystery of why there are no records at the Arnold of Rock's mudan seed or of the plants which surely the arboretum would have raised. (We discount the possibility that the records were among correspondence of the Arnold from 1936 to 1946 destroyed by the then director E. D. Merrill in a "fit of temper".) The first hint of an answer came from the check-lists that accompanied the consignments sent from the Arnold to Kew and Edinburgh where the three lots of mudan seed do not have collection numbers. This explains why they are missing from the original handwritten, numbered notes that Rock sent back with all the other collections. Apparently, Rock took with him a set of notebooks with pre-numbered pages in which to record the details of each collection. The mudan were not included, presumably because they were collected from a cultivated rather than a wild source. However, we know from the typed version of the notes that were sent out from the Arnold to Kew, Edinburgh and presumably the other recipients, that Rock did send brief notes about the peonies, which must have been separate from his field notes. What happened to those brief notes? A plausible explanation is that Sargent took some of the mudan seeds home and took Rock's brief notes along with the seed. He was known to have taken home seeds that he considered were of horticultural rather than scientific interest and when Judd's letter came to light confirming that Charles Sander, Sargent's gardener, had raised two plants from the original seed there was an at least plausible answer to the mystery. There is another possibility differing slightly from this explanation. The information about the mudan seed could have come to Sargent not with Rock's field notes sent with the consignment of seed on December 15th 1925 but as a note included with his letter of December 13th. Then, when arranging for the subsequent repackaging and distribution of the consignment, Sargent also arranged for the recipients of the mudan seed to be given the information he had about it.

Part 3: Germination of Rock's Mudan Seed and the Resulting Plants
Frederick Cleveland Morgan
(1881 – 1962)

We consider in turn each of the known recipients of Rock's mudan seed.

Edinburgh and Kew

As would be expected, different consignments of seed were sent to different recipients. For example, the list of contents sent, along with the 151 packets of seed, to Kew shows only two of the three batches of mudan seed whereas Edinburgh was sent all three among its 148 packets. There seems to be no information on the amount of mudan seed Rock sent to the Arnold or how much of it was sent by Sargent to the various recipients.

Surprisingly, we can find no evidence that any plants were raised at either Kew or Edinburgh. At Kew, there is no record of sowing, although other collection numbers from the same consignment do appear in the propagation records. At Kew there are several plants erroneously labelled *Paeonia rockii* or something similar, but their accession records confirm that none have any direct connection with Rock's seeds. At Edinburgh, there is the pencilled note "Did not germinate", against one of the lots on the contents list but that is all we could find. At Edinburgh, there is an interesting plant labelled *P. suffruticosa* ssp. *rockii,* believed to have originated at Logan (see below), which may possibly be a clonal propagation from an original Rock seedling, but is probably a later seedling. There is no doubt that at least some of the seed was viable since some plants were raised in other places. As the seed coats would have been dry and hard on receipt, it is doubtful if any would have appeared above ground until the following spring at the earliest, so perhaps the seed containers were thrown out too soon; but one would have thought botanic garden staff were experienced enough to know that. However, it should be borne in mind that literally thousands of packets of seeds were pouring in to these places each year and it is understandable that some may have been neglected or not even sown at all.

Rothschild, Saunders and Havemeyer

We have no knowledge that plants were raised by Rothschild, Saunders or Havemeyer. It might have been expected that Professor Saunders, an acknowledged authority and breeder of both tree and herbaceous peonies would have been successful, but in his many contributions to the American Peony Society Bulletin right up to the time of his death in 1953 there is no sign that he was. If he had raised plants, he surely would have used them in his breeding programme and there is no evidence of this as far as we know.

Charles Sargent

The two plants that Charles Sander raised and flowered in Sargent's garden at Wollaston, Massachusetts have given rise to their own mysteries. Sadly, Sargent died in 1927 so would not have known of Sander's success. The two plants must have first flowered in 1932 or 1933, as Judd, in his letter to Morgan of the 5th May 1938, refers to having raised a batch of seedlings from them "which are not yet large enough to flower." (Stern, in his monograph, inferred that all the original seedlings first flowered in 1938, another error that has been repeated down the years). Judd's comment about the colour of the petals being pale lilac is interesting, but possibly of limited significance. He may only have been referring to the colour on first opening which is often pale pink before changing to white. On the other hand the flowers may have been bluish pink. In which case this is the only instance of a bluish tinge reported from plants from Rock's seed although it is not especially rare in Gansu Mudan as a whole. Also, we note in passing that Sargent's death was a disaster for Rock because no further sponsorship by the Arnold was forthcoming.

The fate of Judd's (second generation) seedlings has eluded us. There appears to be no record of any finding their way into the Arnold arboretum. It is possible that they were destroyed by rodents, but we have not been able to confirm this. Sargent's estate was sold after his death and has since been built over. The fate of the original two plants is revealed in the letter dated 16th February 1967 in Stern's file at Kew from an amateur peony breeder Leo J Armatys, of Sampson & Armatys, Attorneys at Law, from Central City, Nebraska. At Stern's suggestion he had written to the Director of the Arnold Arboretum "for information as to Rock's Variety", and mentions that he had received "several interesting letters from them". He goes on to say "Their records do show two tree peonies grown from seed sent by Rock from Tibet. One was 481-29, from Sargent's estate and the other was 907-36 from Charles Sanders (sic) – but both plants died". There seems little doubt that these were the two plants mentioned above. The letters from the Arnold to Armatys could be interesting, but we have been unable to find out whether the Arnold still has them.

The Bergius Botanical Garden, Stockholm

We have not visited the Bergius Botanical Garden and, again, have experienced some difficulty in obtaining the definite proof that we would like to see regarding the fate of the seeds sent to them in 1926. For much of what we know we are indebted to Tom La Dell, a landscape designer from Kent who worked at the Bergianska as a student in the 1970's. La Dell became interested in this subject following the article by Stephen Haw in *The Plantsman* (September 1991) where the petals of "*Paeonia suffruticosa* 'Rock's Variety'" were described as "more or less pure white, sometimes slightly tinged pink" (this was based on the plant at Highdown which Haw & Lauener wrongly believed to be *P. rockii* and an original from Rock's seed). La Dell remembered that plants he saw growing in the Bergianska in his student days and which were said to have been raised from Rock's seed, varied from light to dark pink in colour and none was white. This concurs with several reports we have received about pink-flowered plants of 'Rock's peony' in other gardens in both Sweden and Norway, although we suspect that 'pink' could equally mean 'not pure white' or 'blended pink and white'. La Dell returned to the Bergianska in October 1991 and examined the accession records which showed that six plants had been raised from seed received from the Arnold Arboretum in 1926, of which four were still living. The most recent (2005) information we have is that only two, or possibly three, still survive. Critically, the records also show the origin of the seed to have been the "Prinsens av Choni trädgården" (the Prince of Zhuoni's garden). We have seen only copies of the (typed) records, which are not actual contemporaneous records, so we are unsure whether the information about the Prince's garden did come with the packets of seed sent from the Arnold to the Bergianska. However, it is the most likely answer and we have no reason to doubt that it did. Then of course it is no surprise that the resulting flowers were various shades of pink because two of the three seed lots were from plants in the Prince's garden with 'red' and 'white' flowers. Like the plant(s) in the lamasery garden, but even more so because of the different colours, the plants in the Prince's garden were very probably Gansu Mudan and not *P. rockii*.

Whether they were derived from the batch of seed from the red-flowered plant (which was likely to have been some shade of pink), or from the white-flowered plant the two (and there may well have been more than just those two) would almost certainly have cross pollinated. Karl Evert Flinck, the respected Swedish horticulturist, in a letter to Tom La Dell dated 21st May 1992, reports that "I have planted probably a thousand seeds (from the Bergianska plants) over the years and never had any white flowering plants. There have been plants that have flowered very pale but not clear white as the Rock form does (sic)". This would be curious if the information, in Rock's brief notes, about the flower colour of the seed parent plants could be taken at face value because even if the white colour was recessive, one would expect it to appear eventually. But just as 'red' might not mean what we might instinctively understand then so might not 'white'. We have evidence from a catalogue of the Bergianska nursery dated 1939 that plants raised from seed taken from the six originals have been distributed since at least that year and this no doubt accounts for many of the the pink-flowering Gansu Mudan to be found in Scandinavian gardens today.

Berlin-Dahlem Botanic Garden

Our information about over thirty Gansu Mudan at Berlin-Dahlem has come from our friend Irmtraud Rieck who contacted, among others, Gärtnermeister Rolf Marquardt, a retired former curator of the botanic garden. It seems that the wooden shelves carrying what remained of files of historic records after extensive wartime damage became infected, probably with dry rot, and in 1974 both the shelves and the files were burnt. There appears to be no documentary evidence at Berlin to connect the mudan there with Rock's seed. Marquardt's opinion, received, he says, from his predecessor Stenzel, is that they are (directly) from Rock's seed. According to Marquardt, "It has always been the case that the plants here today, at least seventy years old, are of the first generation Rock provenance and none are of the further offspring sown later in European, American or New Zealand gardens". If this view was accepted then Berlin would have not only have had highest germination rate of any of the recipients of Rock's seed, but also has by far the highest number of surviving plants today and by far the widest range of flower colour. A detailed report prepared by Marquardt in May 2002 indicates that the thirty or so plants with single flowers and with the characteristic blotches vary from pure white to wine-red; the colour of the anther filaments also varies from white to 'red' and there are examples where the sheath colour is 'red'. The wide variation in colour indicates extensive hybridity, possibly involving Feng Dang group plants.

Whatever the details of their origin and whether or not they are all over seventy years old we have no doubt that all these plants, like those at the Bergianska are not *P. rockii* but examples of Gansu Mudan.

Cleveland Morgan

Of the characters in this saga, Frederick Cleveland Morgan is, in horticultural circles, the least known; yet the significance of the part that he played cannot be over-estimated. Even Stern, despite receiving his plant from him never referred to him by name in any of his published writings. In fact the only clue as to his identity comes from a hand-written note on Stern's garden record card for the plant, then referred to as *Paeonia suffruticosa*.

Cleveland Morgan was a wealthy businessman, a son of James Morgan and eventually vice-president in the family business of Henry Morgan and Company (known as Morgan's). He had a country estate at Senneville on the Island of Montreal, Canada much of which became in 1945, due to Cleveland Morgan's initiative, about half of the Morgan Arboretum of McGill University. He collected fine art from all over the world and was largely responsible for establishing the Montreal Museum of Fine Arts, and for most of its exhibits. He studied botany, embryology, geology and zoology at Cambridge University and might have gone on to a career in natural sciences had not his eyesight been inadequate for microscope work due to a childhood accident. He was well known as a horticulturist, particularly for his interest in rock gardening and as a breeder of bearded iris and orchids. It may have been through irises that he initially made contact with Stern. Exactly when they first met is not known, but they were both present at a conference on, ironically, "Rock Gardens and Rock Plants" in London on May 5th, 6th and 7th 1936, organised jointly by the Royal Horticultural Society and the Alpine Garden Society, where Morgan gave a paper entitled "Rock Gardening in the Province of Quebec". It was probably at this conference, or during the dinner on the Tuesday evening, or perhaps in the hotel bar afterwards, that Stern first learned of Morgan's involvement with `Rock's peony'. Stern had presumably by then begun work on what would become his famous monograph and it is perhaps not too fanciful to imagine his astonishment as, out of the blue, he suddenly discovers that growing in a garden in Canada is what he assumes is Farrer's legendary peony and additionally that small plants had been produced. Whatever actually took place it cannot be a mere coincidence that he duly received a specimen of the peony "from a friend in Canada as quite a small plant in the autumn of 1936" (JRHS, 1959). Also present at the conference was G. P. Baker, a leading figure in horticultural circles at the time, a former President of the Alpine Garden Society and an expert on Iris, which would have linked him with Stern. He too received, presumably from Morgan, a mudan plant, which proved to be similar or identical to Stern's plant. The note on Stern's own record card confirms that the donor was "Cleveland Morgan of Montreal" and the date as November 1936. He also noted on his record card that "Dr Rock tells me he collected it in summer of 1926"!

Details of the outcome of Rock's seed sent from the Arnold to Morgan in 1926, remain obscure. It is hard to believe that Morgan kept no horticultural diaries or notebooks, but despite help from several people in Quebec none have as yet been located, although there are plenty of records and correspondence of his fine art activities. However, by good fortune and the interest and diligence of Céline Arseneault, the librarian at Montreal Botanical Garden, a letter dated January 27th 1941 from Morgan to Henry Teuscher, the garden's designer and first curator, was found in the Teuscher archives there. The two were apparently in the habit of exchanging plant material and in this letter Morgan wrote "The few seeds of Peony suffruticosa are worth trying as it is very rare and only now becoming known. I grew my **one plant** from seed sent me by the Arnold Arboretum and collected by Rock in Tibet over ten years ago". This shows Morgan probably knew the correct date of his receipt of the seed and it seems unlikely that he would not have given Stern accurate information, which makes Stern's subsequent errors about the original seed from Rock all the more inexplicable. Here again the solution of one mystery leads to another. There is no mention by Morgan of the flower colour of his plant although we assume it must have been white, more-or-less. On the other hand the two seedlings raised by Sander and said by Judd to be "from the same lot" were described as lilac coloured. If there was literally only one plant how was it pollinated to produce viable seed? Morgan's granddaughter Elizabeth Morgan, who still lives in the old family home, 'Le Sabot' in Senneville, has confirmed that the plant no longer exists there. The "quite small plant" that Morgan sent Stern is believed to be the large shrub still flourishing in Stern's old garden at Highdown, near Goring-by-Sea, Sussex.

Kenneth McDouall (1870-1945) of Logan, Scotland

Logan, a sub-tropical garden a few miles north of the Mull of Galloway, became part of RBG Edinburgh in 1969; prior to that it had been owned privately. The garden was effectively created by Kenneth McDouall and his brother Douglas during the first half of the last century. McDouall was an outstanding plantsman, well-known in his day. He sponsored the expeditions of contemporary plant hunters such as E. H. Wilson and would have acquired new plants from many sources. McDouall was not on the list of recipients supplied by Judd and the only published indication of his involvement comes from a remark by Stern in the December 1939 article he wrote for the JRHS. In his letter to Stern Rock says "If you have any seed to spare of this beautiful *Paeonia*, I would appreciate if you would send me a few seeds by registered letter to ensure their arrival. I should like to plant them in my garden." In his article Stern relates that he did send Rock some seed, not from his own plant but from McDouall, but omits any information about the source of McDouall's seeds. Instead he writes "It may be interesting to record that seeds of this Paeony kindly sent to me by Mr K. McDouall of Logan, were sent to Dr Rock in China to replace the plants destroyed in the Lamasery at Choni and were safely received by him, so let us hope the Paeony will again bloom in the lamasery in years to come to bring peace and joy to the monks.". This flight of fancy may have some appeal for uncritical romantics but is actually nonsensical. The destruction of the Lamasery, however thorough and even by fire would not necessarily and not even probably have destroyed the peonies in the garden. Much more plausible is that if they had been destroyed it would be because they were dug up for danpi.

The Plant Database of the Royal Botanic Garden, Edinburgh, under the name *Paeonia suffruticosa* S. G. Haw (the author should be Andrews), includes five specimens under their accession number 19599781 which are stated to have been wild collected in China by Joseph F. Rock (another error). Four of these are growing at Logan and the other at the main garden in Edinburgh. This latter plant, which is said to have originated at Logan, was moved to its present site in 1987 from the garden of Professor D. M. Henderson, former Regius Keeper, when he retired. We have been told that when RBG Edinburgh took over Logan there were no records relating to the garden and its plants and that the only evidence of the origin of the mudan came by word of mouth from the older staff there. There is no evidence in their dispatch records to suggest that Edinburgh was the source,

either as seed or seedlings, of McDouall's mudan and hence to connect the Logan plants with the Arnold Arboretum and Rock. Having seen the plants at Logan in flower in 2003, we thought they were slightly pinker than usual and turned to the Bergianska as a possible source, but still could not find the link. Finally, a misfiled letter in Stern's papers at Kew provided the answer. It was the second of two letters from Kenneth McDouall to Stern dated May 9th and 16th 1938. The first letter accompanied two blooms of "Rock's Peony (sic)....to show colour variation". In the second letter McDouall wrote "The seed of this peony came from Wilson, from America. It was collected by Rock whom I remember described it as a beautiful species with a large flower. The seed was taken from a plant growing in a monastery garden which Rock came across on a collecting expedition in China. I do not know the year but it was some time ago. I do not think the seed had a number when it came here." Wilson was working for Sargent at the Arnold when Rock's seeds arrived and obviously knew McDouall. In fact, Barrie Unwin, the current curator at Logan, has confirmed that Wilson is known to have visited Logan. Here yet again an answer leads to more questions. How could McDouall have remembered in 1938 that Rock described 'the peony'? Did Wilson send seed to McDouall with Sargent's knowledge; which batch or batches did it come from; and did Wilson send any elsewhere? McDouall's May 9th letter appears to be in response to an enquiry from Stern and, together with his subsequent supply of seed to Stern, seems to imply that at that time McDouall had at least two fairly mature plants. After McDouall's May 16th letter Stern wrote to Edinburgh B.G. seeking information and only after drawing a blank there wrote his letter to Goodspeed which was forwarded to Rock.

We have seen the four plants at Logan and in our opinion, judging by their present size and locations, they are unlikely to be the originals raised from Rock's seed. The one at Edinburgh looks from its size to be much older, but is still most unlikely to be an original plant. It may have been a seedling from an original, or even perhaps a layer or rooted cutting from one, but it is unlikely that this can ever be determined. One thing is fairly clear though, Kenneth McDouall at

P. `Highdown' at the Highdown Garden in late May

Chris Sanders with the original plant of P. `Highdown'

P. `Highdown' at the Highdown Garden

An atypical leaf with rounded leaflets and no red colouring taken from the original plant of P. `Highdown' at the Highdown Garden.

Individual flowers on the original plant of P. `Highdown´ at the Highdown Garden

Bottom row: Two flowers and a leaf taken from the plant of P. `Highdown' in Chris Sander's garden

Logan has the honour of being the only person in the UK to grow and flower plants from Rock's original seed.

This review of the few plants known to have resulted from the original seed distributed by the Arnold Arboretum shows that only the two or three survivors at the Bergianska in Stockholm can be considered to be 'originals' although at least some of those at Berlin very probably are. In the absence of any absolute proof of vegetative propagation from an original seedling all the other plants in cultivation today known as Rock's Variety or something similar are from second or subsequent generations (or totally different sources). They must therefore be regarded as Gansu Mudan, belonging to *Paeonia* Gansu Group, as indeed so must the few originals. We hope we have proved conclusively that there is no justification for the use of the name *Paeonia rockii* for such plants and it should not, therefore, be used in future.

Part 4: The Highdown Plant(s) and propagation of 'Rock's peony'
Frederick Claude Stern
(1884-1967)

Stern, eventually, Colonel Sir Frederick Stern, is chiefly remembered for the Highdown garden and for his two best-known works, *A Study of the Genus Paeonia,* published in 1946, and *Snowdrops and Snowflakes* published in 1956, both of which are now much sought-after collectors' books. However his early life in particular was more colourful than this might suggest. As a young man he spent some time big-game hunting in Africa and also rode as an amateur steeplechase jockey. After he married in 1919 he and his wife Sybil began creating a garden in an old disused chalk pit at Highdown in Sussex on a south-facing slope of the South Downs. They experimented with many kinds of plants to find out which would do well on a chalk soil and he wrote about their experiences in *A Chalk Garden* (1960). Lady Stern left the garden to Worthing Borough Council for the enjoyment of future generations of gardeners. Many of the trees, shrubs, perennials and bulbs they planted are still doing well nearly forty years later.

Stern wrote many articles on diverse genera, but he was particularly interested in Lilies, Irises, Peonies and Snowdrops. Peonies, in particular, proved to be very successful on the Highdown chalk and many have survived up to the present day, including 'the Highdown plant', the (assumed) original plant received from Cleveland Morgan, which grows near the western edge of the garden. It first flowered in 1938, less than two years after planting and specimens taken from it on May 10th that year are preserved in the Kew herbarium. Haw & Lauener (1990) refer to "two specimens grown from Rock's seed cult. in the garden of F. C. Stern at Highdown" as if there were two plants involved, but this is clearly another mistake. There are actually three herbarium sheets at Kew and as there is no evidence that Stern had acquired other Gansu Mudan at that time they must be assumed to be from the same plant. By 1943 the plant was six feet high and "smothered with bloom" according to Stern, who submitted a vase to the RHS at Vincent Square on May 18th which was awarded a First Class Certificate. The records show a second vase was shown on the same occasion by G. P. Baker of Sevenoaks, which was jointly awarded the FCC. Both were submitted under the name of *P. suffruticosa*. The only information on Baker's entry form reads "It is said that it comes from Tibet". Presumably the two entries were at least very similar for the committee to make a joint award. There is a herbarium specimen taken from Baker's plant, dated 26th May 1940 at Kew. In Stern's file at Kew there is plenty of correspondence between Stern and Baker on irises, peonies and other, mostly bulbous, subjects, but no mention of mudan. While there is no documentary evidence that Baker received his plant from Morgan our guess is that both he and Stern were promised a plant at the same time in 1936 and both plants arrived later that autumn. Baker's old garden in Sevenoaks has long since been built on and we have found no information about the fate of the peony.

One important detail that remains unresolved is whether the plants which Morgan sent to Stern and Baker were seedlings from the single plant raised by him or clonal material such as rooted cuttings, layers, divisions or even grafts. As ten years had elapsed since Morgan first received seed from the Arnold there would have been just enough time for his plant to have produced seedling offspring that would have been old enough to have flowered themselves by 1938. We know from the letter to Teuscher referred to earlier that seed was set and this seems to be the most likely source of the young plants sent by Morgan. This would make the Highdown plant two generations removed from the seed collected by Rock, thus, in our view, eliminating the faintest possibility of its having species status. In fact, there is additionally ample morphological evidence to indicate that the Highdown plant is a Gansu Mudan and not *P. rockii*. Firstly, the filaments of the stamens are heavily flushed with a similar blackish-purple colour to that of the blotches at the base of the petals. In all the pictures of true *P. rockii* and the actual flowers we have seen the filaments and the sheath are white or pale yellow and all contemporary Chinese descriptions we have seen of wild plants of *P. rockii*, including that in the new *Flora of China*, confirm this character. On the other hand in Feng Dan/*P. ostii, P. spontanea (P. jishanensis), P. qiui* and many Central Plains mudan the filaments and sheath are entirely or mostly dark purplish-red. Secondly, there is a tendency for one to several narrow extra petals to be produced in some blooms and this is a further indication, by no means conclusive in itself, of the hybrid status of the Highdown plant.

'Rock's Peony' in North America

According to Don Hollingsworth and Roy Klehm most if not all the plants of 'Rock's peony' that have been propagated in North American nurseries derive originally from scions imported from Highdown by the late David Reath of Reath's Nursery, of Vulcan, Michigan. We have not so far been able to discover the exact date of the importation, but plants (probably grafted) were first offered for sale (as *P. suffruticosa* var Rock's) by Reath in 1971, so it was probably sometime in the mid-late 1960s. Their catalogues at that time said it was the hardiest of all their mudan, coping well with winter temperatures down to minus 29 degrees Centigrade. There is an interesting, but probably misleading statement by Reath in a list of Peonies for Hybridising dated 1979 which

included `Rock's peony´. In this list 'Rock's Peony' was said to be "extremely fertile by selfing". As mentioned earlier there is a widely held belief in the UK, and confirmed elsewhere, that isolated plants do not produce seeds, although we have occasionally heard reports to the contrary. It is very difficult bordering on impossible to prove conclusively that plants are not self-infertile and equally, in many of the cases where seed has been produced, to prove that cross pollination could not have occurred somehow.

Between 1969 and 1972 scions were supplied by Reath to the Klehm Nursery of Barrington, Illinois, who began selling plants grafted onto roots of herbaceous peonies around 1975. Klehm received at least two clones from Reath, one with single and one with double flowers. The emergence of Klehm's double form and the fact that Reath obtained seed from his plants suggests to us that in the scions sent to Reath several clones were likely to be involved that could have come from 'random' seedlings at Highdown.

Propagation from the Highdown plant(s)

There seems to us little doubt that some, possibly a quite high proportion, of the mudan grown in British gardens today as 'Rock's Variety', 'Joseph Rock' etc., or more recently and regrettably as *Paeonia rockii,* have descended directly or indirectly from the plant(s) at Highdown, mostly by means of successive generations of seedlings. The first mention by Stern that he raised seedlings does not appear in print until he stated in *A Chalk Garden* (1960) "Seed of this plant has been raised and comes true." By "true" he presumably meant that the resulting flowers were all basically white with dark blotches, not that they were all identical. It is also probable that he kept and sowed some of the seeds sent to him from Logan in 1938, indeed this is the only possible source for which there is evidence of Gansu Mudan plants to pollinate the Highdown plant (it could have been pollinated by Central Plains hybrids of course). There are several Gansu Mudan growing at Highdown today which, from their appearance, could be seedlings from the Highdown plant or from McDouall's plants at Logan. There are two different plants growing at Kew which the accession records show were donated by him, one in 1943 and the other in 1953. Neither are the same as the Highdown plant and both are presumably seedlings. Stern was known to be a generous gardener and would have given away spare plants to friends and visitors. In this way plants would have been spread around and no doubt successive generations of seedlings have been raised from them and further distributed. From 1940 to 1960 Thomson and Morgan catalogues sometimes offered plants and/or seed usually listed as 'P. suffruticosa - Moutan Peony'. The descriptions fit that of Gansu Mudan and sometimes are explicit about variable colour and form. Some of the seed offered is believed to be from the Highdown plant. Terry Dick in Aylesbury has two flourishing plants from this source, both white, one noticeably double, and he has distributed seedlings germinated from the seed they set.

All the seedling plants that have been produced, in gardens or commercially, will show differences from one to another. Whilst most will retain the essential characteristics of a so-called 'Rock's peony', namely large, white or pink-flushed or pink flowers, single or with varying degrees of doubling, with dark basal blotches differing in colour and shape, some will clearly show Central Plains/Suffruticosa characteristics. All those with appropriate features should be referred to as Gansu Mudan or, more formally, as members of *Paeonia* Gansu Group. None are *P. rockii*. We are sure that this rather sweeping statement applies much further afield than we have been able to see at first hand. We are conscious of labels saying *P. rockii* or 'Rock's Peony' in gardens, botanical and otherwise, in thousands of places unknown to us. Our challenge to all their custodians is "Prove it; but whether or not there is any presumed connection with Rock, read this account first".

The Highdown plant has been propagated vegetatively by cuttings. There is a note on Stern's record card that two cuttings were rooted in 1956 and planted out in 1958. Neither of these appears to be present in the garden today. The late Graham Stuart Thomas grew a plant in his last garden at Briar Cottage, Kettlewell Close, Woking which he told one of us (C.S.) originated as a cutting from the Highdown plant and on subsequent comparison it appeared that the two were identical. Contrary to what is often written, it is possible, with care, to root cuttings, (see Chapter 7).

On the other hand there is a good deal of evidence that the Highdown plant has been increased by grafting, at least in the UK. Notcutt's Nursery of Woodbridge, Suffolk was probably the first to be involved. According to Frank Knight, a former managing director of the company and later a director of the Royal Horticultural Society's garden at Wisley from 1955-1969, in a letter published in the NCCPG Newsletter No. 5 for Autumn 1984, scions from the Highdown plant were grafted using the roots of herbaceous peonies as understocks in February 1951. The agreement was that the resulting plants were Stern's and in due course were despatched to recipients of his choice. How long this arrangement continued is not clear but there is evidence that Notcutt's continued to propagate the plant for their own customers in small numbers until at least the early 1960s. Knight mentions in his letter that seedlings of *P. delavayi* were also used as understocks, but that there were problems with suckering. It never found its way into the firm's catalogues, however, and the demand always exceeded the supply. Ivan Dickings, a retired former head propagator for the company continues to graft a few plants from time to time and often uses *P. delavayi* seedlings as understocks.

There is an old specimen of 'Rock's peony' growing in the Dry Garden at the Savill Garden in Windsor Great Park and their records show that it was received as propagation material from Highdown in 1960. The following year plants were sent from Windsor back to Highdown and to Kew although as far as we know these do not exist at either garden today. Because of the short time-span we can assume that the plants must have been grafted, even in the absence of any direct evidence. At the RHS Garden at Wisley, Surrey, there is a large plant growing in the wild garden which is recorded as having been received from Windsor in 1973, although there is apparently no corroborative record at Windsor. Scions from this plant were grafted onto herbaceous peony roots by Ivan Dickings in the mid 1990s and two plants were returned to Wisley in 1996 and are now growing well in the Hot Borders. We have examined these plants in flower and all appear to be identical with the Highdown plant.

A leaf of P. `Joseph Rock'

Paeonia `Joseph Rock'

Individual flower of P. `Joseph Rock'

Above left and right: Individual flowers of P. `Joseph Rock'

The Present Situation:
Paeonia 'Highdown' and Paeonia 'Joseph Rock'

Probably the only person producing grafted plants of the Highdown clone commercially in the UK at the present time is Peter Catt of Liss Forest Nursery in Hampshire, albeit on a very small scale. His stock plants originate from the Graham Stuart Thomas specimen referred to earlier. Rather unusually, Peter Catt uses root sections of *P. delavayi* as understocks to avoid problems from suckering. A ten-year-old plant from this source is growing strongly in Chris Sanders' Eccleshall, Staffordshire garden. It is currently nearly two metres high and bore over thirty flowers in 2005. It has never produced viable seed.

The Klehm Nursery, now run by Roy Klehm and called Klehm's Song Sparrow Perennial Farm and Nursery has its main site at Avalon, Wisconsin. Their catalogues have listed their single flowered clone under various names, first as 'Rock's Variety', later changing it to 'Joseph Rock' and then *P. rockii* (syn P. 'Joseph Rock') and in the illustrations they have used the appearance of the flower has varied, just as the appearance of flowers of the Highdown plant in different publications has varied. Most recently it has been listed simply as P. 'Joseph Rock'. There have been several thousands of examples of this clone produced which probably makes it the Gansu Mudan clone most extensively known to have been vegetatively propagated. (It is impossible to say with confidence what might similarly have happened in China.) It would be a neat conclusion to this complicated account if the Highdown plant and Klehm's 'Joseph Rock' plant were the same clone but they definitely are not. Our first-hand experience of the Klehm plant is mostly limited to two young plants received from Roy Klehm that have not yet flowered, and two plants that remain from a batch Klehm sent to Sissinghurst in the early 1980's one of which is now growing in a garden in the Cotswolds. All have an identical and distinctive foliage characteristic, notably broader, thicker and somewhat overlapping leaflets which lack the early bronze-red tinting present in the Highdown plant and many others. Some pictures of the Klehm plant flowers closely resemble a photograph which appeared in an article by Sir Peter Smithers in *The Garden* for November 1992 which he described as "the (sic) plant distributed in the USA, propagated vegetatively…." but there was no discussion or illustrations of the foliage. Minute examination of the edges of petals and blotches of individual flowers of Gansu Mudan will always reveal variations but attaching great significance to such variations is misguided.

The relationship between the Highdown plant and the Klehm plant is unclear and will remain so even if more detailed information about what material was sent to Reath and subsequently what material was sent to Klehm is ever found, and in any case it is essentially inconsequential. Both clones are simply examples of Gansu Mudan, two amongst many hundreds, and as the pictures in Section Three show, not such exceptional examples. The factors that make them both important are their places in the story of Gansu Mudan, especially the Highdown plant, and the extent to which they have been vegetatively propagated and distributed, especially the Klehm plant. These factors lead to the necessity of validly published cultivar names.

Paeonia 'Highdown' and Paeonia 'Joseph Rock': 'New' Cultivar Names for the Highdown and Klehm Plants

The Highdown plant has been referred to by various authors in the past as 'Rock's Variety' and as 'Joseph Rock', but neither appears to have been validly published as its cultivar name. As a result, these names have been used indiscriminately for anything that vaguely resembles a 'Rock's peony', i.e. a Gansu Mudan with 'white' flowers and dark basal blotches. Since the general acceptance of *P. rockii* as a species, albeit with complications discussed in Chapter 3, this name, depressingly, seems to have taken precedence over both cultivar names possibly for commercial reasons. As horticultural journalists utilise the romance or mystery of the inaccurate versions of the story of 'Rock's Peony' to make a more interesting article and fail to separate it from true *P. rockii* (which they have almost certainly never seen) the kudos of the species name increases.

The earliest publication of the name 'Rock's Variety' that we have found was in a note from Stern in the JRHS for August 1959. However, although it is clear that he was writing about the original plant, he did not describe it, merely stating that "it seemed to be exactly like the wild tree paeonies described by Reginald Farrer" even though Farrer did not actually describe the crucial characteristics of the wild plants. In any case the word `Variety´ contravenes Article 19.19 of the International Code of Nomenclature for Cultivated Plants (I.C.N.C.P.) 2004, thereby invalidating the name. Exactly when or who first coined the name 'Joseph Rock' is not clear but it has been in use at least since 1984 when an article by Diana Grenfell entitled *Paeonia suffruticosa* 'Rock's Variety' appeared in the Spring Newsletter of the NCCPG. In it she used the former name interchangeably with the latter and further confused the issue by referring to several plants in other gardens as well as the Highdown plant without making it clear if she was treating them as a single clone or not. Cameron Carmichael, in the Spring 2001 issue of *Plant Heritage,* did his best to clarify matters by proposing that "the only plant that should be called 'Joseph Rock' is the FCC plant." However, the description accompanying the article is incomplete and there is no photograph or reference to a herbarium specimen, so we doubt if this constitutes proper establishment of the name under the I.C.N.C.P. and in any case Klehm's use of the name predates this article. As we have described above, the name 'Joseph Rock' has been used in the USA for the most extensively clonally propagated clone, and this clone is distinct from the Highdown plant. To use 'Joseph Rock' for anything other than the single-flowered clone propagated and distributed by Klehm would add yet another layer of confusion to an already chaotic situation, so we propose *Paeonia* 'Joseph Rock' as the cultivar name for that plant. For the Highdown plant, in our view the most satisfactory way out of the nomenclatural tangle is to wipe the slate clean and start again with a new cultivar name. The most obvious and logical choice of name is *Paeonia* 'Highdown' so we propose that this name is given to what is generally assumed to be the original Gansu Mudan at Highdown and to all and only its vegetative descendants.

For a publication to validly establish a cultivar name a written description is required even though such a description (in this context at least) can be used only negatively, to deny the name to a particular specimen, although it could be argued that the published description effectively defines a 'group cultivar name' - i.e. if a specimen fits the description it can take the name whatever its origin. On the other hand even clonal examples could differ in appearance if grown in different circumstances. This problem is discussed elsewhere and will continue to be a problem whatever is said and decided about it. We avoid it here by stating that the primary criterion for valid use of *Paeonia* 'Highdown' and *Paeonia* 'Joseph Rock' is provenance - the certain knowledge that they are clonally propagated from authentic specimens, and that the pictures and descriptions here are additional to that criterion.

It may be helpful to repeat here that in a cultivar name and the formal descriptions below the latin form of a genus name, here Paeonia, and an unambiguous common name of a genus, here Peony, are both valid and are to be regarded as equivalent.

Description of *Paeonia* 'Highdown'

The basic description is a white, single flowered Gansu Mudan, category 1.1. in Section 3. However neither 'white' nor 'single' here are absolute so 'category 1.1 or just possibly 1.2 or 9.1 or 9.2' is more helpful. From a horticultural point of view there are several features which, although each is present in many other Gansu Mudan, collectively are a useful aid to its identification, at least in the negative sense: the young foliage in spring is more or less suffused with a reddish-bronze colour which gradually reduces as the season progresses, but is still present to some degree at flowering time (probably reduced if the plant is growing in shade); the colour of the outer surface of the petals in the bud stage is pale pink and this shade shows on the inner surface on opening, but quickly becomes white (less quickly in shade); there are 10 or 11 normal petals, about 12 cm wide by 10 cm long borne in the usual two whorls; in addition there may be one to several extra strap-shaped staminoidal petals; the inner blotches are oval-shaped, deep blackish-purple in colour, feathered lighter at the edges, up to 4.5 cm long by 3 cm wide; there are faint back blotches (see 6.1 (vi)); there are up to 300 filaments borne in a dense mass; the inner, most visible filaments are heavily stained almost the same colour as the blotches, except for a short white base and a little more white near the anthers; the outer or lower filaments are more or less white; the 5 green carpels have creamy-white stigmas and are initially enclosed by a cream-coloured sheath which splits open as they mature; flowers are moderately and pleasant scented, reminiscent of roses. Once established, P. 'Highdown' can grow quite rapidly and is capable of forming a rounded shrub up to 2 m high and 1.5 m wide in ten years.

Description of *Paeonia* 'Joseph Rock'
The basic description is a white, single flowered Gansu Mudan, category 1.1 in Section 3. Particular features which, although each is present in other Gansu Mudan, collectively are a useful aid to its identification, at least in the negative sense are: the foliage is almost always uniformly deep green, the leaflets are almost all lobed and pointed and the lower leaflets nearest the rachis on each of the main pinnules overlap; there are usually 10 normal white petals borne in the usual two whorls with no or very little pink colour; the petals are quite broad at the base so the blotches on the outer whorl are mostly obscured; the blotches are oval-shaped, deep blackish-purple colour, feathered lighter red-purple at the edges, up to 4 cm long by 3 cm wide, there are usually faint back blotches; the filaments are mostly white, red-purple at their base; the 5 green carpels have cream-white stigmas; the sheath is cream-white; flowers are moderately, pleasantly and typically scented. Once established on its own roots P. 'Joseph Rock' can grow strongly to form a slightly upright rounded shrub about 2 m high in fifteen years.

Postamble
Our investigation into the story of 'Rock's Peony' began with plants - hundreds of Gansu Mudan, none of which were *P. rockii*, and fewer, but still many, labelled or claimed to be *P. rockii* all of which were Gansu Mudan. This was not clear at first of course. What started as a suspicion and rapidly became a total certainty was that what botanists and horticulturalists were saying about *P. rockii* and 'Rock's peony' was inconsistent and self contradictory. As we tried to extract scraps of evidence from all the received wisdom and uncritical and unthinking repetition of nonsense, two experiences became familiar. One was that nothing, no matter who had said it, could be accepted without testing and corroboration. The other was that even in the most dubious statements there was likely, if we came back to it often enough, to be a loose flap of darkness which could be lifted up to find some light

Some remaining uncertainties seem capable only of speculative clarification but we believe that evidence may well exist about:

i) Cleveland Morgan's plant: a description of it; what was propagated from it and hence what was sent to Stern and Baker; what happened to it; was there really only the one plant and if so what pollinated it.

ii) Reath's propagating material from Highdown: who actually collected and sent it and when; what did it consist of; what did Reath produce from it and how, and what was distributed.

iii) Judd and his seedlings: what was the source of Judd's list of recipients; did any of Judd's second generation seedlings flower and what happened to them.

iv) Recipients of Rock's mudan seed: are there others we have not discovered and are there any more original seedlings that we do not know about?

ACKNOWLEDGEMENTS

A number of people have kindly helped us in various ways to unravel the tangled threads of the story of Rock's peony. We would especially like to thank the following:

Céline Arseneault, Chris Beardsley, Chris Brickell, Cameron Carmichael, Peter Catt, Anne Chambers, Paul Cook, Sarah Cook, Veronica Cross, Lindsay D'Aoust, Alexis Datta, Terry Dick, Ivan Dickings, John Elseley, Mark Flanagan, Karl Flinck, Maurice and Rosemary Foster, Chris Grey-Wilson, Don Hollingsworth, Reiner Jakubowski, Roy Klehm, Sybil Kreutzberger, Hermann Krupke, Tom La Dell, Alan Leslie, Kenneth Lorentzon, Ron Macbeath, Rolf Marquardt, Diana Miller, Elizabeth Morgan, Rolf Nilsson, Martin Page, Irmtraud and Gottlob Rieck, Eric Schmitt, Claudia Schroer (APS), Pam Schwerdt, Bill Seidl, Mike Sinnott and Barry Unwin. Also the staff at the RHS Lindley Library, the Arnold Arboretum, RBG Edinburgh, RBG Kew and the Bergius Botanical Garden, and the Trustees of RBG Edinburgh and RBG Kew for permission to reproduce archive and herbarium material.

REFERENCES

Allen, T. (1984). The Pollination of Paeonia suffruticosa – *NCCPG Newsletter* No.5

Armatys, L. (1967). Letter to Stern (No.5) in Stern, *Paeonia* mss. at RBG Kew.

Carmichael, C. (2001). Joseph 'Rock's peony' – *Plant Heritage* **8** (1): 8.

Chittenden, F. J. (ed.) (1936). Rock Gardens and Rock Plants. Report of the Conference Held by the RHS and AGS May 5th, 6th & 7th.

Chock, A. K. (1963). J. F. Rock (1884-1962) – *Taxon* **X11** (3): 89-102.

Farrer, R. (1914). *The Gardeners' Chronicle* 1448, 26th September 1914

Farrer, R. (1917). *On the Eaves of the World,* London, Arnold

Grenfell, D. (1984). Paeonia suffruticosa Rock's Variety – *NCCPG Newsletter* No. 4

Halliwell, B. (1984). *Paeonia suffruticosa* 'Joseph Rock' – *NCCPG Newsletter* No. 5

Haw, S. G. (1985). Mudan: the king of flowers – *The Garden* **110** (4): 154-159.

Haw, S. G. (1986). A Problem of Peonies – *The Garden* **111** (7): 326-328.

Haw, S. G. & Lauener, L. A. (1990). A Review of the Infraspecific Taxa of *Paeonia suffruticosa* Andrews – *Edin. Journal of Bot.* **47** (3): 273-281.

Haw, S. G. (1991). Tree Peonies: A Problem Resolved (sic) – *The Plantsman* **13** (2): 94-97.

Haw, S. G. (1993). Letter in *The Garden* **118** (4): 176.

Haw, S. G. (2001). Tree Peonies – A Review of their History and Taxonomy – *The New Plantsman* **8** (3): 156-171.

Judd, W. H. (1938). Letter to F. C. Morgan (No. 180) in Stern, *Paeonia* mss. at Kew.

Judd, W. H. (1938). Letter to F. C. Morgan (No. 181) in Stern, *Paeonia* mss. at Kew.

Knight, F. (1984). Propagated at Notcutt's – *NCCPG Newsletter* No. 5.

McDouall, K. (1938). Letter to Stern (No.227) in Stern *Miscellaneous* mss. at Kew.

Morgan, D (1992). *The Morgans of Montreal* 209pp - Private publication, Toronto.

Morgan, F. C. (1938). Letter to Stern (No. 179) in Stern, *Paeonia* mss. at RBG Kew.

Morgan, F. C. (1941). Letter to Henry Teuscher in *Teuscher* at Montreal BG.

Palmer, The Hon. Lewis (1967). Col. Sir Frederick Claude Stern OBE, MC, FLS, VMH – *Journ. Roy. Hort. Soc.* **92**: 379-381.

Rheder, A. & Kobuski, C.E. (1933). *Journ. Arnold Arboretum (Arnoldia)*.

Rock, J. F. (1924-1927). Various unpublished mss. and numerous letters from Rock
http://www.arboretum.harvard.edu/library.tibet/search.html

Rock, J. F. (1924-1927). Original diaries covering the expedition to Kansu in the archives of RBG Edinburgh.

Rock, J. F. (1925). Field Notes in the accession records at RBG Kew and RBG Edinburgh.

Rock, J. F. (1925). " Experiences of a Lone Geographer: An American Agricultural Explorer Makes His Way Through Brigand-Infested Central China En Route to the Amne Machin Range, Tibet." – *National Geographic Magazine* **XLV111:** 331-347

Rock, J. F. (1928). " Life among the Lamas of Choni: Describing the Mystery Plays And Butter Festival in the Monastery of an Almost Unknown Tibetan Principality in Kansu Province, China." – *National Geographic Magazine* **L1V:** 569-619.

Rock, J. F. (1930). "Seeking the Mountains of Mystery: An Expedition on the China-Tibet Frontier to the Unexplored Amnyi Machen Range, One of Whose Peaks Rivals Everest" – *National Geographic Magazine* **LV11:** 131-185

Rock, J. F. (1933). "Land of the Tebbus" – *National Geographic Magazine* **LXXX1:** 108-127.

Rock, J. F. (1938). Letter to Stern (No. 179) in Stern, *Paeonia* mss. at RBG Kew.

Rock, J. F. (1939). Letter to Stern (No. 210-211) in Stern, *Paeonia* mss. at RBG Kew

Sargent, C. S. (1926). Standard letter to all recipients of Rock's seeds in accession records at RBG Kew and RBG Edinburgh.

Smith, W. W. (1941) Letter (from Edinburgh B.G.) to W. T Stearn and copy sent to F. C. Stern

Smithers, P. (1992). 'Rock's peony' – *The Garden* **117** (11): 519-521.

Smithers, P. (1993). Letter in *The Garden* **118** (4): 176.

Stern, F. C. (1939). The Moutan Paeony – *Journ. Roy. Hort. Soc.* **64:** 550-552

Stern, F. C. (1956). *A Study of the Genus Paeonia* – London, RHS.

Stern, F. C. (1959). Paonia suffruticosa Rock's Var. – *Journ. Roy. Hort. Soc.* **84:** 366

Stern, F. C. (1960). Tree Paeonies – *Journ. Roy. Hort. Soc.* **85:** 295-299

Stern, F. C. (1960). *A Chalk Garden* – Edinburgh, Nelson.

Sutton, S. B. (1974). *In China's border provinces; the turbulent career of Joseph Rock, botanist-explorer* – New York, Hastings House.

Wagner, J. (1992). From Gansu to Kolding – The Expedition of J. F. Rock in 1925-1927 and the Plants Raised by Aksel Olsen – *Dansk Dendrologisk Årsskrift* **X:** 19-87.

Wagner, J. (1993). Letter in *The Garden* **118** (4): 176.

Wu, Z., Raven, P. H. and Hong, D. Y. (eds), Flora of China, Vol. 6 2001 (Paeonaicae), Science Press, Beijing & Missouri Botanical Garden Press, St. Louis

5a. GENETIC FINGERTPRINTING EVIDENCE
Ben Davis, Mike Fay and Will McLewin

To examine the relationships between some of the cultivated and wild Mudan discussed in Chapters 3 and 5 a genetic fingerprinting study of 13 examples was carried out at the Jodrell Laboratory, Royal Botanic Gardens, Kew by Ben Davis and Mike Fay.

Genetic fingerprinting involves the production of a set of fragments which reflects the genetic constitution of an individual plant. These fragments can be characterised as bands in gel electrophoresis using radioactivity, silver staining or fluorescent dyes to label the DNA.

Earlier methods of genetic fingerprinting required relatively large amounts of DNA and, hence, also a large quantity of leaves, but techniques developed in the 1990s incorporating the amplification technology of the polymerase chain reaction (PCR) allow fingerprinting studies to be carried out with much smaller initial samples of DNA. In 1995, a technique called 'amplified fragment length polymorphisms' (AFLP) was developed by Keygene Inc. (Vos et al. 1995) and is the most sensitive fingerprinting technique currently available suitable for use with plants for which specific techniques have not been developed. The technique has several advantages over other currently used fingerprinting methods:
1. It is fast (the technique has been automated);
2. It requires relatively small initial quantities of DNA;
3. It provides 10-100 times more interpretable fragments and is thus more sensitive than some other fingerprinting techniques;
4. It is highly reproducible.

For these reasons, AFLP was chosen to investigate the genetic diversity in the Mudan samples in a blind study with the examples numbered randomly. In the AFLP fingerprints 98 bands could be identified. Of these 70 (71.4%) were present in every sample, indicating that all the samples are closely related. The remaining 28 bands were absent from 1-12 of the samples. Parts of representative traces are shown opposite together with a tree derived using the neighbor joining cluster algorithm showing the relationships between the samples. Branch lengths in the tree give an indication of genetic distance.

All the samples had unique fingerprints at this level of sampling. The three samples from plants of wild origin, 8, 12 and 13, were the most genetically distinct and were distinct from the samples from plants in cultivation. The six samples directly or indirectly from Highdown were found to be genetically very close but P. 'Highdown' and P. 'Joseph Rock' were found to be distinct. Samples 1, 4 and 5 were indistinguishable as were samples 9 and 11. Sample 10 possessed one band only not found in 9 and 11. It should be pointed out, as the traces suggest, that the technique requires some active interpretation together with skilled judgement about which peaks to accept. The reliability of the technique is probably higher than the 95% claimed by Vos et al and so the study confirms the thrust of the previous Chapters in Section 1.

Right:
Sections of sample traces from the AFLP reactions, showing some shared and some varied DNA fragments (represented by the peaks). The numbers on the scale are the length in base pairs of the DNA fragments. Some fragments varying between samples are indicated by arrows.

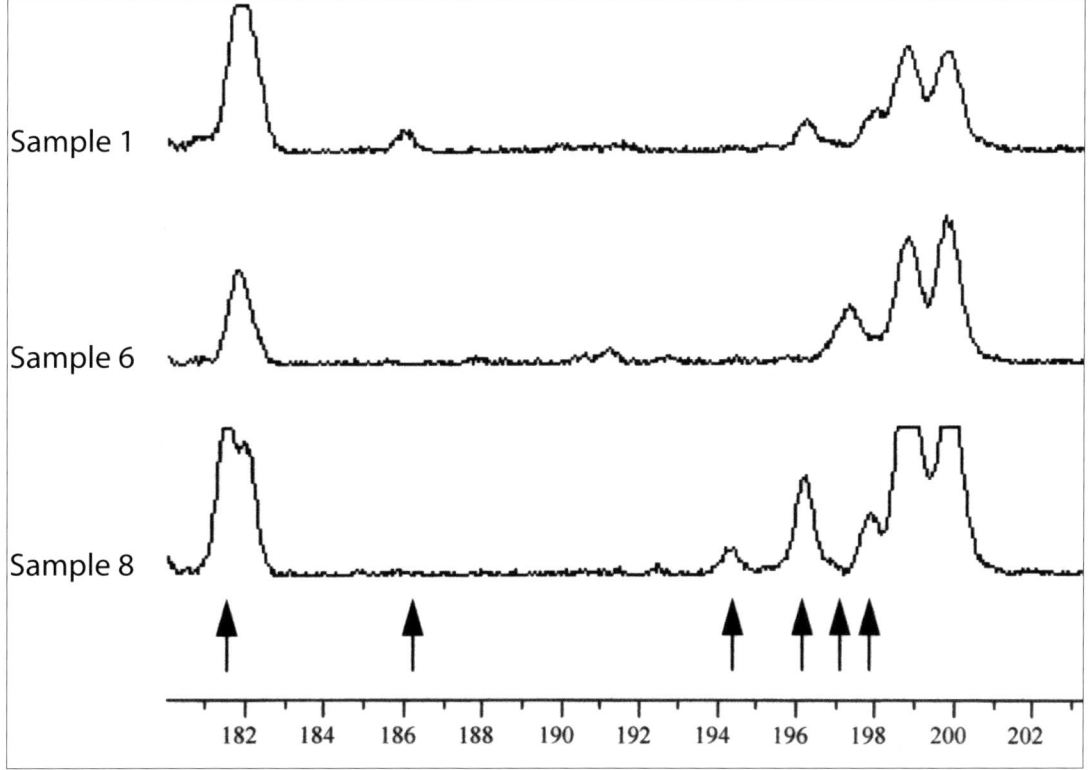

Provenance of samples:

1. The large Gansu Mudan at the north end of the order beds at R.B.G. Kew believed to be a seedling from P. 'Highdown'
4. Chris Sanders' Gansu Mudan believed to be vegetatively propagated from P. 'Highdown'.
5. F.C.Stern's original plant of P. 'Highdown' still flourishing at Highdown.
9. Young grafted plant of P. 'Joseph Rock' from Klehm's nursery.
11. Young grafted plant of P. 'Joseph Rock' from Klehm's nursery.
10. The mature plant of P. 'Joseph Rock'; one of the batch sent to Sissinghurst in 1980's.
6. The white double flowered Gansu Mudan distributed by Klehm.
2. A Gansu Mudan at Picton's Nursery near Worcester.
3. A mature Gansu Mudan at Phedar Nursery received as 'Siemans form of P. rockii'.
7. The mature Gansu Mudan at Ness Botanic garden (see page 38).
8. P. rockii from Wen Xian
12. P. rockii from Tianshui (E)
13. P. rockii from a location in Tianshui (E) distinct from that of 12.

Vos, P., Hogers, R., Bleeker, M., Rijans, M., Van de Lee, T., Hornes, M., Frijters, A., Pot, J., Kuiper, M. & Zabeau, M. (1995) AFLP: a new technique for DNA fingerprinting. Nucleic Acids Research 23: 4407-4414.

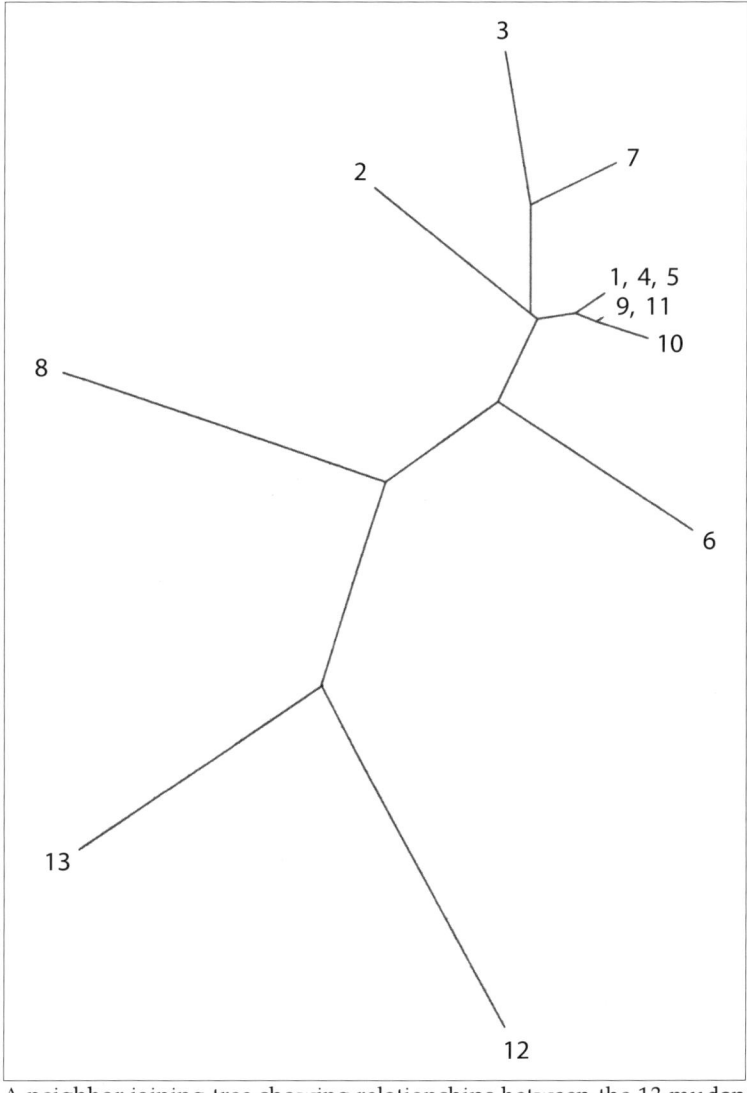

A neighbor joining tree showing relationships between the 13 mudan samples.

玉龙杯

Paeonia Gansu Group ‘Yu Long Bei’

SECTION 2

PLANTS AND NURSERIES

---

6. BOTANICAL AND HORTICULTURAL FEATURES OF GANSU MUDAN

6.1 Morphology

In common with many large groups of hybrid plants overall appearance and particular features vary greatly between individuals and can be significantly affected by the micro- and macro-environment. Nevertheless there are some noteworthy general characteristics.

The stronger and more vigorous examples can, in time, grow to over three metres in height and width. Such specimens, or even more-usual mature plants one to two metres high and as wide, free flowering and with the usual upright or outward facing flowers can reasonably be described as magnificent.

A detailed comparison between P. rockii, Gansu Mudan and Central Plains Mudan at Peace Peony Nursery, Lanzhou, Gansu is in Section 1 Chapter 4, p.38.

(i) Roots
(ii) Buds
(iii) Branches
(iv) Leaves
(v) Flowers
(vi) Blotches and Back-blotches
(vii) Fruit and Seed

(i) Roots

The woody quality of the roots is greater than that of other mudan. The danpi (the root bark) of Gansu Mudan is not as thick as other mudan so in this respect they are much less productive than, for example, the Feng Dan plants that are grown extensively in Jingnan – south of the Yangtze River. Also there are more side roots and fibrous roots than other varieties of Mudan. This feature presumably aids their survival in various adverse environments. The roots of Gansu Mudan can reach several metres deep down in the loose, soft and deep loess soil at Peace Peony Nursery, where ten-year-old Gansu Mudan seedling plants with 7mm thick roots at a depth of three metres can

Top left and right, above: Initial leaf and bud growth, in some cases hairy in others not.

Early spring growth on a grafted plant that has been deeply planted.

have strong Feng Dan influence the new branches are more pithy, less brown and more green-white in colour and are not as reliably frost hardy.

(ii) Buds

Gansu Mudan produce leaf buds and flower buds. In general leaf buds are thin and small and flower buds are large and fat, but it is not always easy to be sure which buds are flower buds. Small flower buds are more likely to be those of flowers without normal stigmas and stamens. Both tip buds and axillary buds can be flower buds. When flower buds develop they produce a stalk bearing 5-7 compound leaves and the flower comes at the tip. In favourable circumstances a seedling will produce flower buds after 4-6 years.

Tip flower buds of Gansu Mudan can be as large as 1.0cm (bottom diameter) by 2.8cm (length) and are usually larger than those of the wild *P. rockii*. Axial flower buds have a narrow base and are generally smaller. The colour of the flower buds

A Gansu Mudan in early Spring, with normal or the most common form of branch growth.

Upright form of branch growth.

Spreading form of branch growth.

changes during their development: green to brown in early summer and autumn, more reddish-purple in spring and more green again as the flower opens. To some extent bud shape and colour can be used to identify different varieties in autumn and winter.

(iii) Branches

Gansu Mudan generally have strong main stems, 15 cm in diameter is possible in old plants. The wood of the main stem and branches is hard and there is not much pith. The phloem or inner bark is relatively thin and the epidermis or outer bark is dark grey-brown. New branches are a light brown colour. The angles of branches and the shapes of Gansu Mudan vary greatly, reflecting the different groups of plants involved in their development. Where the influence of Central Plains Mudan is very strong (equally, in Central Plains Mudan even with some Gansu Mudan influence) there is a tendancy towards several pithy main stems which are damaged by drought and cold and which re-grow from the base.

A Gansu Mudan seedling with entire (unlobed) leaflets. It would be *P. rockii linyanshanii* form if it had come from true wild seed. This plant is at the late infancy stage and has made very strong new branch growth for the first time.

Gansu Mudan showing both pointed and more rounded leaflets.

An established Gansu Mudan with broad unlobed leaflets.

(iv) Leaves

Gansu Mudan have large bi-pinnate leaves which give them an attractive appearance before and after flowering time. Overall leaf size varies greatly. Main leaves, those not on the new growth of a flower stem, can be over 30cm long and 25cm wide with a 15cm petiole.   Individual leaflets are a mixture of deeply lobed, shallowly lobed and (rarely) unlobed. Lobes may be rounded or pointed. Generally leaves are dark or bright green above and light green or grey-green beneath. Sometimes the edge of a leaflet is pale brown, occasionally dark brown. Leaf size and leaf colour are affected greatly by the environment and the cultivation conditions. The leaf veins on the underside of the leaf stick out and are hairy. In general the more hairy the underside of the leaves the greater is the plant's resistance to cold.

Bottom left and right: Gansu Mudan leaves showing various leaflet shapes and colours.

Left and above: Spectacular autumn leaf colour in Gansu Mudan in pots and probably partly induced by stress.

Autumn leaf colour at various stages in Gansu Mudan in pots.

The new young leaves just developing are brightly coloured and very attractive. At this stage they are sometimes conspicuously hairy and so they catch and retain water droplets after rain or watering. The glittering effect this produces is as eye-catching as display of spring flowers. Autumn leaf colour can be spectacular but is unpredictable

Left: Young Growth of Gansu Mudan in Spring, after rain.   Right: Early autumn leaf colour in an established Gansu Mudan growing in open ground.

Top row and above: Examples of Gansu Mudan flowers showing the different appearance that results from different petal shape. When petals are   broad at the base and overlapping the blotches of the outer whorl are obscured. When petals are narrow at the base and not overlapping there appears to be a single ring of ten blotches. In between the two extremes alternate blotches appear as narrow spikes.

A Gansu Mudan flower with back blotches. The blotch colour is present on both surfaces of the petals.

(v) Flowers

While the range of identifiable flower forms of Gansu Mudan is not quite as large as that of Central Plains hybrids almost anything is possible in terms of the degree and form of doubling.

In bud the ornamental part of the flower is enclosed in three round-shaped sepals. The more outer two are green and the more inner one whitish initially. Immediately beneath the sepals are three narrow bracts of an involucre. These are very variable in size and shape, usually narrow and 3 –6 cm long but sometimes like a small pinnate leaf. The sepals and the bracts persist after petals have fallen and seed ripened. Inside the sepals the petals, carpels and stamens sit on a woody disc. The carpels are initially enclosed in a sheath, a membrane attached to the disc. Some authors persist in referring to this sheath as the disk, which is particularly perverse and unhelpful. The sheath colour is white (or yellowish white) in all wild Gansu Mudan, red-purple in Feng Dan plants and mostly some sort of red in Central Plains hybrids. Consequently the sheath in Gansu Mudan can be any of these colours. Almost exactly similar remarks apply to the filaments.

Gansu Mudan flowers with dark back blotches. The blotch colour is present on both sides of the petals. Right: An example of white back blotches; the inner blotches are black.

Examples of Gansu Mudan with different colour flowers on the same branch. Usually this effect is the result of the intesity of pink colouring reducing as the flower ages.

In partial and full double examples the extra petals inside the bowl of 'normal' petals are (in most cases) the result of petalization of some or all of the up to 300 stamens. Some or all of the filaments become petaloid to a greater or lesser degree (from 3 to 25 mm in width). In some cases the anthers remain and produce pollen. There are also examples where the stigmas have become petaloid. In many examples the precise form or the degree of doubling can vary slightly or markedly from flower to flower on the same plant and from year to year. In particular early flowers may be more double than later ones during the flowering season and flowers overall may become more double as plants become well established and grow strongly. The 'normal' outer petals are round or fan-shaped, sometimes heart-shaped. They can be smooth edged or frilled.

(vi) Blotches and Back-blotches
The most striking and distinctive character of Gansu Mudan is of course the dark blotches at the base of the petals. These can vary from a delicate smudge to a large thumbprint; they can be neat or ragged edged or flaring out into the petal; they can be solid or hollow. They can be any colour from black through purple to crimson and red. They can be black edged crimson and so on. (They can even, rarely, be absent. In this case the designation of the plant as a Gansu Mudan is somewhat debateable and rests on its provenance and the other characteristics of the Gansu Group.)

However to be precise the familiar blotches should be called inner blotches, or, to translate literally from the Chinese, belly blotches, because plants have been developed at Peace Peony Nursery with pronounced outer or back blotches – blotches on the back of the petals. The phenomenon of back blotches has been unreported in the previous thousands of years of peony culture, presumably because until recently although back blotches have existed, albeit rarely, they have been small and insignificant. The presence of a white blotch on the back of the petals of a dark pink or purple coloured flower is not uncommon but the black back blotches on pale coloured petals is previously unremarked on.

Gansu Mudan fruit at various stages of ripeness.

Even after the seed has gone the empty seed pods are attractive.

The development of strong back blotches has great significance because they exhibit the characteristic feature of Gansu Mudan whichever way the flower is seen. This feature and its effect should not be confused with that of seeing the 'shadow', in bright light, of the inner blotches from the outside of the flower. The inner blotches and the petal shape interact to affect the internal appearance of the flower. When petals are wide at the base there are five blotches visible. When petals are sufficiently narrow at the base ten blotches are visible, a very different effect. In intermediate examples between each blotch is a spike of colour from the partly obscured blotch beneath.

Gansu Mudan flowers, especially single forms, where the inner blotches are most striking, are usually carried upright.

(vii) Fruit and Seed

Single-flowered Gansu Mudan normally bear fruit well and so do most lotus and rose types. More complex doubles on the whole bear little or no fruit, nor do those that flower very late or plants whose pistils fail to develop well. Most if not all Gansu Mudan are self incompatible so isolated plants will rarely if ever produce viable seed. In general the seed pods of white flowers are quite smooth, usually pubescent and pale yellow-green, often with a reddish-brown seam as they develop. The seed pods of dark-coloured flowers are more dark grey-brown and often a bit wrinkled. Usually there are usually five follicles, which bend outwards during development of the seeds to form a flat star when the seed is ripe. At this stage the seed pods split, discharging some or all of the seeds although sometimes there is a sticky secretion inside which prevents the seeds falling and is a nuisance when collecting the seed. One thousand fat seeds weigh about 270gm, so there are 3,500-5,000 viable seeds per kilo. Seeds collected and not needed for sowing can be ground to obtain oil for cooking.

6.2 Features during growth: Annual and Overall Life Cycles

Gansu Mudan have been developed in a continental climate with cold dry weather and with slightly acid, loose and rich soil. However they are very adaptable and can be successfully and easily grown in many different environments.

Annual Life Cycle

The main factor affecting the germinating, initial growth and flowering of Gansu Mudan is the average temperature during the day. The flowering period can vary from year to year by up to 15 days, possibly more.

1. Initial growth period

This is from the first signs of dormancy breaking until the appearance of the first leaves. In early and mid March or earlier the buds start to change colour from brown to reddish and gradually expand. In Lanzhou this is while there are still

Comparison of (average) flowering times of Gansu Mudan between Lanzhou, Beijing, Stockport and Auch				
	Lanzhou	Beijing	Stockport	Auch
Sprouting	14.03-29.03	09.03-19.03	18.03-12.04	20.02-01.03
Early flowering	25.04-06.05	19.04-25.04	03.05-12.05	01.04-10.04
Late flowering	18.05-02.06	03.05- 08.05	28.05-12.06	03.05-13.05
Seed ripe	16.08-12.09	26.07- 02.08	20.08-21.09	25.07-20.08

frosts and before the sap of most of the trees and flowers has started to flow. In Auch and in Stockport where the weather in Winter is unpredictable and much less severe there are signs of new growth in January, sometimes earlier but any leaves that appear before Spring are often damaged by later frosts.

2. New branch growing period

This is the period from the first leaf until new growth stops. Whether new branches (current-year's-growth) grow well or not depends both on the variety and on cultivation and management. Weak growth is common during the first two years after re-planting. After two years of good care, the plant recovers and then grows normally. Branches grow longer and thicker at the same time. Before flowering, the plants usually stop growing taller but horizontal growth stops later.

There are two kinds of new growth of Gansu Mudan: one produces branches with tip buds from leaf buds, the other produces new branches from flower buds. The latter do not produce strong buds beyond the lower part and in winter the upper part of the new growth dries up and shrivels. That is why it is said Mudan 'grow ten cun (about 30cm) and die back six cun'. New branch growth is usually bright red, turning to brown and green, and on flowering shoots stops when flower buds begin to develop. The new branches become woody as the flowers develop, sometimes not quickly enough to hold the developing flower upright.

3. Flowering period

The flowering process can be divided into seven stages:

i) **Sprouting:** mid and late March (at Lanzhou). The hard, dormant bud gradually changes colour and becomes bigger and the bud surface loosens. This period lasts about ten days.

ii) **Bud expanding:** the involucre starts to appear from the bud. If the plant is not strong enough or suffers from cold at this stage, then the bud may not develop further. This period lasts about 7 days.

iii) **Aeolian bells:** mid- and late April, the bud is about 1.2 to 1.5cm in diameter. (Leaves start to open.)

iv) **Round boll:** in early May the bud can quickly become as big as a cotton boll. After this period, buds become flowers according to the characteristics of varieties and the prevailing weather. This period lasts about 7 days.

v) **Early flowers:** this period lasts about 2 to 7 days from the first flower to about 25% of the buds in flower.

vi) **Full bloom:** this period lasts about 6 to 10 days from 25%-80% of the buds in flower.

vii) **Late flower:** about 3-5 days from when 80% of the flowers fall off until all the flowers are gone.

The times from the start of flowering to shedding of all flowers vary with varieties and with environmental conditions. The flowering period will be longer with lower temperatures and will be reduced by high temperatures and by rain during the flowering period. Even when the weather in a particular location is predictable and basically consistent quite small variations can change the flowering time for a particular plant by up to 8 days. Where the climate is unpredictable flowering times can vary from year to year by much more. Gansu Mudan in Beijing flower earlier than in Lanzhou but the flowering period is shorter due to the more rapidly increasing temperature. In Stockport some flower buds begin growth earlier but flowering finishes later due to erratic weather, with warm spells in winter and cold spells after growth has begun. In normal circumstances established Gansu Mudan do not have 'big' and 'small' flowering years.

4. Seed period

During the first 1 to 2 days of flowering, the anthers ripen and release pollen. As the flower opens fully the stigma start to secrete a sticky juice and become receptive. This period lasts 3-7 days or more. Most, possibly all, varieties of Gansu Mudan need cross pollination before they can produce fertile seed. The development of seed may be affected by wind or rain or insecticide spray during the flowering season.

Gansu Mudan bear strong and fat seed. If seed is not to be collected removing spent flowers seems to help plants flower better the next year. In order to get fat, sound seed, it helps to remove excessive, damaged and late flowers, and flowers on weak branches.

5. Leaf fall and dormant period

In late October and early November in Lanzhou leaves of Gansu Mudan to fall. If there is early frost, most leaves will turn yellow or red but do not fall for some time. Autumn colours can be spectacular but are unpredictable. In sustained winter conditions a strange effect sometimes occurs after the first frost, when some still green leaves on late growing branches become frozen and do not fall during the winter.

6. Root growth

Gansu Mudan transplanted in spring can produce new root hairs quickly enough to absorb nutrition and water to support bud and branch development although individual branches may die back. Roots stop growing during branch development and start to grow again after flowering has ended. Root growth speeds up when seed is ripe.

Overall Life Cycle

Gansu Mudan go through three stages from the moment they sprout: infancy, adulthood and old-age. During different stages, there are different cultivating and appreciating features.

Infancy

Infancy of seedlings spans the period from germination to the plants first flowering after 4-7 years. In the first 1-3 years, Gansu Mudan grow very slowly above ground. It is mainly the roots that grow. The plant above ground may be only 4-15 cm tall. In years 4 to 7 the plant above ground starts to grow much more rapidly and may grow as tall as 60 cm, possibly more, and will usually begin to flower, although the form and colour of flowers may not yet be stable. In this period the supply of water especially in Spring is important. With adequate and timely water and a compound fertilizer the infancy period can be shortened.

Adulthood

The adult period of Gansu Mudan seedlings and of vegetatively propagated plants spans from when they start flowering regularly to when the flowering starts to slow down. It can be expected to last about a hundred years. During years 7 to 15 Gansu Mudan grow in size most strongly. New branch growth can (rarely) be as much as 60cm. The colour and form of flowers are basically stable for selection. During adulthood it is necessary only to prune to establish the form of the plant and to remove excessive basal shoots that are not wanted. From years 10 to 100 Gansu Mudan, as tall as a man and as wide, can be relied upon to produce a display of striking opulence without blowsyness that is argueably without equal.

A Gansu Mudan in early adulthood, about 12 years old; established, growing and flowering well and set to display its splendour every late Spring for longer than anyone will live to see it.

Gansu Mudan about thirty years old in fruit. The plants whose growth is unbalanced and being restricted can, if desired, safely be removed and replanted.

Old-age

Gansu Mudan are shrubs of great longevity. Specimens over a hundred years old are still able to regenerate without attention as long as their circumstances remain favourable. However, basic care such as turning over the soil and adding organic fertiliser, removing weak and thin and any diseased branches and maintaining their space becomes important. In Gansu, in Yuzhong, Longxi, Lintao, and Linxia, Gansu Mudan over a hundred years old can be seen still flowering profusely.

An old Gansu Muan. The thickness of the branches is indicated by a pen. Venerable plants continue to flower spectacularly but by this stage their overall size has ceased to increase. Also few shoots come from the base unless there is severe damage to the branch structure.

7. CULTIVATION AND PROPAGATION OF GANSU MUDAN

Both of these topics can be covered briefly because Gansu Mudan are not difficult to grow successfully. There are many plants grown in cultivation that do require specific conditions, particularly plants which originate in extreme environments, but for many plants the compendious instructions sometimes given about cultivation are a poor substitute for a bit of common sense and are more a bizarre source of comfort for the reader than a necessary set of requirements for the plant. Gansu Mudan are very adaptable. Unless the environment is markedly unsuitable or their treatment markedly inappropriate they will grow well.

7.1 Cultivation

    (i) Planting
    (ii) Feeding and Pruning
    (iii) Watering
    (iv) Sunlight
    (v) Transplanting

The ideal situation for Gansu Mudan is in deep, rich, open loam draining well but not particularly fast in a fairly sunny position with brisk air circulation. None of the three collaborating nurseries featured in Chapter 8 and which have experimented with and specialise in growing Gansu Mudan has exactly these conditions, so they are not essential. Obviously the more extreme the deviation from the ideal the less well plants will grow without remedial measures, but on the whole any half-decent site will do.

So, in very loose, sandy soil add plenty of organic matter especially leaf-soil to provide nutriment and aid moisture retention; in heavy sticky clay add grit and again organic matter to aid drainage and encourage root growth.

(i) Planting

For plants on their own roots, simply dig a large enough hole (any shape will do) for the roots to be spread apart and unconstricted. Put the plant in, with the roots spread and at least partly descending and fill the hole burying the roots. Unless the soil is very nutritious some old organic manure mixed in the soil below the roots will be beneficial. Planting depth is not critical – the same as the plant was before or a bit deeper. Aim not to leave air pockets – some (damp) fine soil is useful. If (just to make the point) you want to grow a Gansu Mudan in a crevice between rocks make the best space you can and cram the roots in somehow. In this case choosing a relatively small plant would be sensible.

For grafted plants some extra considerations come into play. The aim with grafted mudan is for the scion to produce own root and for the (herbaceous peony) rootstock to atrophy and rot away. This is the opposite aim of most situations where plants are propagated by grafting, and it might be better to use the term understock instead of rootstock to emphasise this difference. So grafted mudan that have been grown on for a year or two but are still without adequate own root should be planted with the union at least 10cm below the soil surface even if this involves burying buds on the scion. (See 7.2 (ii).)

When transplanting seedlings and young plants there are several obvious things and one unexpected bit of advice to bear in mind. Before replanting, young (one to three year) seedlings may need to be trimmed to remove broken branches and any diseased root. It may be better to remove thin and weak branches from near the base. When shaping and trimming plants aim, where practicable, at slightly less total branch than there is root and to cut branches cleanly a little above a strong outer bud if possible. Give consideration to orientation, usually with the weaker side towards the sun so that balanced growth is encouraged. Do not remove soil

A young Gansu Mudan plant. This is actually a grafted plant about four years old which had adequate own-root when it was first replanted and the understock was removed. The stem colour shows the replanting depth and subsequent new root growth is indicated by the label. The important point to notice is that the total root structure is greater than the branch structure and is more-or-less undamaged in this case. This is an ideal situation, difficult to maintain when larger plants are moved.

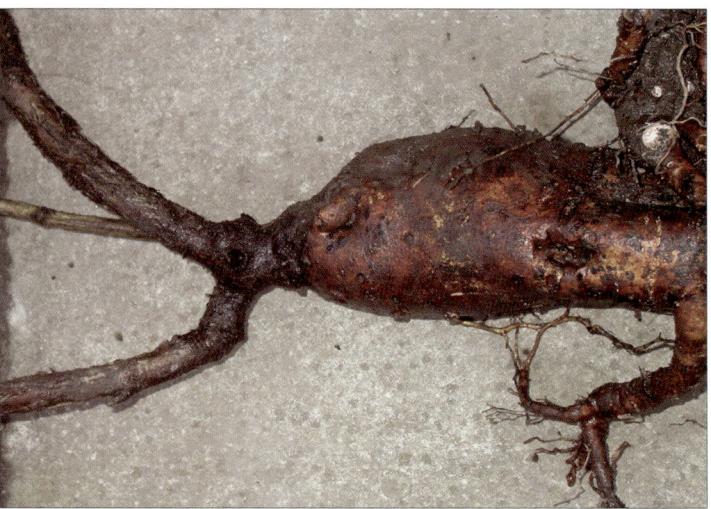

A grafted Gansu Mudan which has not been planted deeply enough and has made no own-root.

around the roots unless there is a need to do so for transportation. Bare rooted seedlings being transplanted can survive seven days exposure in natural light in summer or more than fifteen days in a cool dry dark place even though the root bark becomes shrivelled and wrinkled. Neither is recommended of course. However it is not a good idea to soak the seedlings for long before replanting. It is better to plant them in moist soil and then water at intervals promptly afterwards.

(ii) Feeding and pruning

The starting point in considering these two activities is that in the wild nobody feeds and

A grafted Gansu Mudan which has perhaps been dug up one year too soon. In this case we would remove part of the understock hoping that after replanting what was left would provide some support but would atrophy as the scion own-root developed.

A grafted Gansu Mudan three years old with plenty of own root so that the understock can be removed before replanting in a permanent position.

nobody prunes plants. Consequently if you have an urge to do either then the first question is not what or when or how but why.

In nutritious soil the need is to maintain nutrients, so a bit of almost any general purpose fertiliser will suffice. Bonemeal, calcified seaweed, blood fish and bone are all suitable, so are proprietory fertilisers and/or a mulch of old leaf-soil or old animal manure. The same materials are appropriate for thin, poor soil, where improving the soil condition is the aim so continued addition of organic bulk will be beneficial, as a mulch or lightly dug in. Restricted use of quick-acting

nitrogenous fertilizer in Autumn but some phosphate and potash fertilizer then helps plants to over-winter well and also helps to produce autumn leaf colour.

Die-back of twigs and sometimes even branches is a natural part of mudan growth and if unsightly can be removed whenever convenient. After transplanting some die-back should be expected. Unbalanced or unwanted or awkward growths can also be removed at any time – late Spring or early Summer is the best time for the wound to heal, and just above a strong bud is a useful rule of thumb. This can be combined with cutting flowers for indoor decoration. More substantial branch removal may be desired to improve the overall shape of a large plant or to help new growth to develop. This is probably easiest when there are no leaves so early Spring just as growth is beginning may be the best time. A large Gansu Mudan growing strongly will react well to almost any pruning but such a plant is so magnificent that what is appropriate is cautious, careful sympathetic pruning or none at all.

(iii) Watering
A plentiful, or at least adequate, supply of water in good time is important in Spring and early Summer when most new growth takes place, particularly for young and recently transplanted plants. For established plants this will usually mean actively watering only in exceptionally dry periods. Bear in mind that new root is formed during and following early Autumn so watering then may be appropriate.

(iv) Sunlight
Gansu Mudan grow best in sunny situations. The new growth ripens well and flower buds develop more reliably. However they cope very well with shade provided that the soil is at least decent and there is adequate moisture. Many wild plants of P. rockii grow in quite severe shade and experience dry conditions. In hot, humid and rainy places, especially those at low altitude, Gansu Mudan may suffer leaf diseases in August and September. In high, cold, shady and wet places, it would be better to grown them on slopes facing the sun. In extremely dry and hot places, flowers and leaves are likely to suffer and it would be better to grow Gansu Mudan on shady slopes or on the shady sides of buildings or big trees.

(v) Transplanting

It is frequently said that "peonies do not like being moved". This is nonsense. Apart from pointing out that anthropomorphism about plants is rarely other than misleading, if the plant can be moved without damage of any kind then obviously it can be moved anywhere and any time. Avoiding damage of any kind would require moving the entire plant and its immediate landscape intact, which is impracticable. What usually happens is that some, often most, of the root structure is damaged or broken off when the plant is moved and so the ability of the root system to sustain the state, condition and growth of the branch and leaf structure is impaired. Bear in mind that even when there is no obvious sign of root damage most of the very fine active capillary roots will have been lost. Two things follow from this. The more the root system is damaged the more die-back of branches is likely and also the longer the plant will take to recover its previous state. As a general rule the root system underground is as extensive in size as the visible plant above ground and probably more densely branched, so digging up a large Gansu Mudan will usually inevitably result in the loss of much of its root and almost all of its active fine root. If this takes place during the time of active growth then a significant proportion of the branches and leaves should be removed and the replanting done at once. With care, and if circumstances demand it, Gansu Mudan in flower can be successfully transplanted bare-root. In this case speed and watering before and immediately after moving is advisable.

All that said, the best time for transplanting is late Summer, when leaves are changing colour and beginning to cease activity and before new fine root growth begins. At this time plants can survive for weeks out of the ground even with substantial root loss. Of course such treatment is not desirable but it demonstrates that to move them is not particularly risky. If immediate replanting in the desired position is not possible then temporary planting or heeling in or covering the roots with, for example, damp moss will be beneficial. At the very least store bare-rooted plants in a cool, shady place before replanting. Only relatively small plants move 'as if nothing had happened' but even very large plants, twenty or more years old can be moved fairly easily, albeit with a year

or two to recover and with some die-back. For the first year after transplanting removing flower buds as soon as they begin to develop and paying particular attention to watering and feeding will aid recovery. In particularly hot weather after transplanting it would be beneficial to provide shade and possibly spray with water to prevent leaves drying off.

Three Gansu Mudan seedlings in early April in their second year of leaf growth, cultivated in large clay pots.

Detail of the above group: a single seedling plant.

7.2 Propagation

All the traditional methods of propagation are viable options. Micropropagation has been successful in an experimental context and doubtless in time both this and tissue culture will be used for commercial propagation.

    (i) Seed
    (ii) Grafting
    (iii) Division
    (iv) Layering
    (v) Cuttings
    (vi) Micropropagation and Tissue Culture

(i) Seed

No special treatment is necessary to ensure germination. Planting seed when it is fresh, fairly soon after harvesting, will usually give the highest germination rate but seed that is several years old can also give high yields if it has been carefully stored (cold and dry). Simply plant Gansu Mudan seed a few centimetres deep in good quality soil or seed compost and leave outside through the Winter, with precautions against mice and voles if necessary. If seed is planted in open ground or in large pots then after germination it can be left until well established. Usually a root forms after the first winter and the first leaves after the second winter. Artificial cooling in a refrigerator can be used to mimic the effect of two winters outside and thereby save one year of waiting. Breaking the seed surface with a knife blade or with glass-paper before planting to facilitate the ingress of moisture may be worthwhile. Usually a single isolated plant will not produce viable seed. Where there are two or more plants and seeds are allowed to develop and are not collected self-sown seedlings will occur (unless the seed is eaten by mice or squirrels). Seedlings planted out (after one or two summers growth) in a favourable situation and with enough space (30cm spacing is enough) can be expected to flower two to five years later.

(ii) Grafting

This is the usual method for large-scale clonal commercial propagation and is usually done in August or September using root sections from (mascula/lactiflora type) herbaceous peonies as the understock. This grafting system, possibly unique to peonies, differs from that for other woody plants in that the understock is intended to be temporary. It provides supporting nourishment for the scion until the scion forms its own roots. Hence the use of 'understock' here instead of the more usual 'rootstock'. For the scion to make its own roots the union should be at least eight centimetres below the soil surface when planted, preferably more. Side wedge grafts onto herbaceous peony tubers as rootstock is the traditional and most common method. Side wedge grafts are used because usually the thickness of the scion is significantly different to that of the root section and a side wedge is the easiest way to make good contact between the

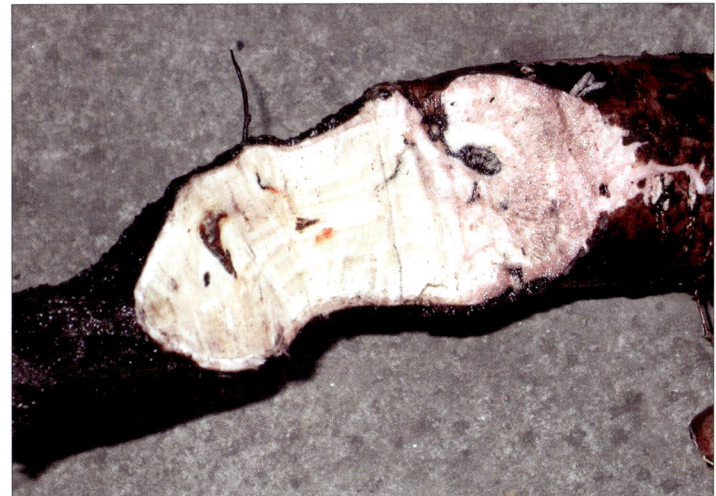

The successful union of a two centimetre thick scion and slightly thicker understock after one side has been removed by sawing. In spite of the apparently perfect fusion we would have doubts about the ultimate viability of the plant unless the scion were to make its own roots.

critical inner bark layers although this may not be so important in this context. Details of the process such as scion and understock size, securing and sealing the join, treatment immediately after the union is made and subsequently, varieties to use as understock and so on vary greatly and seem to be more a case of local convenience and individual experiment than of necessity.

The unions should have calloused after about the fifth week. Ideally the scion makes own-root during the first one to three years and the understockstock atrophies. In some cases the understock grows on and this may be seriously detrimental. The appearance of herbaceous peony shoots, if it happens, is not in itself a problem because they are easily removed. However there is some evidence from our own experience that the scion and understock are ultimately not compatible. Continuing growth of the understock appears sometimes to inhibit the growth of own root by the scion. We have seen large plants flowering and apparently growing well die back completely over two or three years. When examined they have been found to have a large herbaceous rootstock and very little own root. Consequently we would recommend that grafted plants are planted deeply and then dug up after two to four years and the understock removed if it is still present. This will be unpalatable advice for many people though in fact it is not difficult and not very risky. The obvious remedy is to plant mudan that are on their own roots to begin with.

A vigorous Gansu Mudan about sixteen years old. The extent of the root loss is indicated by the sole undamaged root on the right, so although this plant is ideal for division the resulting plants/pieces will need two or three years to re-establish and begin growing strongly.

Seedlings of P. delavayi or P. ludlowii are sometimes used as rootstocks for conventional grafting. Shoots or suckers from such rootstocks can be a problem as they may be more vigorous than the scion. One might just as well use seedling Gansu Mudan but we are unaware of this having been done. Using only the root sections of such plants as rootstock may avoid the problem of suckers but to obtain root sections large enough to match scions requires growing the rootstock plants for unacceptably many years.

(iii) Division

Almost all Gansu Mudan once well established and growing strongly will produce new shoots at the base some or all of which may will develop into branches. These usually come directly from the main trunk even when they appear well to the side. The part of these branches that is beneath the soil surface will develop roots and they can be severed and grown on as a new plant. This is occasionally easy to do but usually much less straightforward than it seems. If the shoot comes from near the surface it may not have enough root. If it comes from lower down it is not so easy to remove without damage. Basal shoots on Gansu Mudan are almost always from the main branches and not from part of the root system as they are likely to be with Central Plains/Suffruticosa hybrids, and shoots which are not well rooted themselves often fail to grow on. 'Division proper' of the whole plant when dug up and the roots washed is usually less haphazard.

It is not possible to generalise about this method of propagation because although the extent to which an established plant can be pulled apart into viable pieces is often not obvious until the whole plant is dug up, but large plants rarely grow with a single stem and can usually be pulled apart. Sometimes a large plant

The plant above after ,maximal' division. There are fourteen pieces of greatly varying shapes and sizes. Division to this extent is not necessarily recommended. Not all these pieces will survive although in this case one could be optimistic about most of them. Some of the existing branch growth should be removed but which parts and how much is not obvious. In many cases division is a two stage process taking several years. The divided pieces are grown on and the survivors trimmed and reshaped as and when there is new growth and they have re-established.

A Gansu Mudan cutting sixteen months after being taken. One of several successfully rooted by Chris Sanders. The compost surface after potting was above the lower buds.

A hormone rooting powder was not used but two short vertical slits were made in the bark at the base of the cutting. The evidence is inconclusive but it appears that there may be more root growth from the two slits than elsewhere.

breaks apart as it is being extracted to produce two or more elegant and perfectly viable plants which will grow on without much die-back. Sometimes large or small pieces cannot be separated with enough root and fail to survive or a very awkward shaped plant results which needs time and cutting back to produce something you want to live with. And of course the original plant has gone. Using very small new shoots with little root is effectively a form of micro propagation. It is relatively unsuccessful unless the tiny divisions are treated with care.

(iv) Layering
This is essentially a more cautious form of division. If part of a branch can be fixed below the soil surface it will usually develop roots and can be severed after two or three years and grown on. The buried part can be pegged to prevent movement but holding it down with a stone is better because it conserves moisture near the surface. The outcome is not entirely predictable. Sometimes the whole branch dies back, or the buried section to the tip

dies back. This is more likely when the branch cannot easily be bent into position. Sometimes a longer period is needed for adequate root to form. Cracking or wounding the branch where it is buried may be beneficial but it is not necessary. We never do it so we have no evidence from carefully controlled comparisons. For specimens with a spreading habit of growth this is usually the simplest method of clonal propagation.

There is an extreme form of layering, conveniently called 'trenching' that is sometimes appropriate, particularly for specimens with an upright habit. Here the whole plant is dug up and buried horizontally in a shallow trench a few centimetres below the soil surface. After two or three years the buried branch or branches will have rooted along their length and vertical shoots from nodes or buried buds will have developed. These small plants can be simply separated and grown on by cutting the original branch, possibly in situ without lifting the whole of the original plant. When this technique works well it is profoundly satisfying. Occasionally of course the buried plant dies. This is immensely disappointing. Survival during trenching seems to be more likely when the branch tips are left exposed but doing this sometimes results in fewer shoots developing from underground. Here again, our comments are not based on careful, extensive, controlled experiments but summarize the outcome of ad hoc experiments.

(v) Cuttings

This is essentially the extreme form of division in that the severed pieces have no roots at all and consequently need much greater care to grow on successfully. Equally it is an extreme form of micropropagation.

Although widely discounted as a propagation method, particularly by commentators who have not tried it seriously, hardwood (or semi-hardwood) cuttings can be rooted and grown on to clonally increase Gansu Mudan. A procedure was described in the 'Gardener's Chronicle', October 26, 1946 by Collingwood Ingram. Chris Sanders has recently been successful with a simpler procedure but using a heated propagator. The aim is to maintain an environment in which the cut twig survives to produce roots by the Autumn. The basic details are mid-summer new growth cut just into older wood; substantial but not total leaf reduction; some bottom heat but warm to cool ambient air temperature; quite high but not excessive humidity; a very porous but moisture retentive rooting medium for example mostly perlite with some peat; transfer to a growing-on compost the following Spring as top growth begins.

It is fair to say that mudan cuttings do not root as readily as most plants for which cuttings are the standard propagation method and that care is needed, particularly with the 'rooting environment'. The easiness of the grafting process once the necessary preparations for rootstock have been made and its reasonably high success rate even in rough and ready circumstances probably explains why cuttings are rarely used. This in turn explains why there has apparently not been extensive experimentation to determine the optimal timing and treatment for what is essentially a much simpler process.

(vi) Micropropagation and Tissue Culture

The laboratory process of producing tiny plantlets from small shoots or from minute scraps of parent tissue in an artificial sterile medium is in itself nowadays not difficult. More problematic is growing them on to a viable size and ensuring that they subsequently develop well and grow normally. A successful regime for micropropagation of what was probably a Gansu Mudan was devised at Wye College in Kent in the late 1980s. Some of the plants produced flowered after 2-3 years. The details can be found in a paper in the *Journal of Horticultural Science* (1991) 66 (1) 95 - 102 by Harris, R.A. and Mantell, S.H.: Effects of stage II subculture durations on the multiplication rate and rooting capacity of micropropagated shoots of tree paeony (*Paeonia suffruticosa* Andr.)

8. NURSERIES AND PEOPLE

Three nurseries are involved with this book about Gansu Mudan. But the involvement is unequal. The history of Peace Peony Nursery begins around 1961 when it was started by Chen Dezhong and its story, until now, is essentially his story. His adventures and unremitting effort devoted to his aims of greening bare landscapes and developing a group of tough, versatile mudan to use for that purpose (and others) could be the subject of a book in its own right. Instead we outline his story and in Section 3 let his achievement, the plants themselves, now becoming increasingly widespread and important, speak for him. Will McLewin at Phedar Nursery and Robert Pardo at La Pivoine Bleue have collaborated with Peace Peony Nursery since 1997 by experimenting with and testing Gansu Mudan in greatly different environments and growing regimes and by helping to demystify these legendary plants and introduce them in Europe. They share with Chen Dezhong a passionate enthusiasm for Gansu Mudan and for Mudan as a whole rather than the commercial production of particular varieties. They also share with Chen Dezhong a profound career change. They all left their established professions to get deeply involved with plants, particularly peonies, both for study and to make them more widely available.

Chen Dezhong and Chen Fuhui.

Will McLewin and Chen Dezhong at Peace Peony Nursery.

8.1 Peace Peony Nursery

In autumn, 1961, responding to the government's call for 'educated urban youth to go and work in the country and mountain areas to strengthen agriculture', Chen Dezhong resigned from his position of accountant for a factory workshop in Lanzhou City. He returned to the poor and drought-stricken district of his home town of Peace, determined to plant trees and shrubs to clothe barren hillsides. He studied at home to obtain a college degree in farming and forestry, became a senior forestry engineer and in 1967 began to build what became the Peace Peony Nursery. He experimented with, introduced and propagated trees suitable for the climate and barren hills of Northwest China. At the same time he began to develop new varieties, and in time a new group, of large-flowered, vigorous, versatile and tough mudan for the same purpose. He collected the old varieties of purple-blotched mudan from local areas, wild species mudan (now called *P. rockii*) from higher altitudes, introduced from Shandong and Henan varieties of Central Plains Mudan and began a long programme of inter-breeding.

In the early years of the nursery he explored the nearby hills and valleys in order to solve the water problem. Through the course of ten winters he managed to dig a self-flowing underground channel 150 metres long through the mountain to bring water to the nursery. To overcome the lack of light in the working tunnel he used ordinary mirrors to divert natural light. His exploration of wild peony species has continued, with field studies in provinces and regions such as Gansu, Shanxi, Shaanxi, Hubei, Henan, Sichuan, Yunnan, Tibet and the northeast of China. These many expeditions often involved hunger and hardship but, together with experience growing and observing all the Chinese herbaceous and woody peony species at the nursery, they have given him a depth of first-hand knowledge of them that is unmatched by that of the many authors and academic botanists who have commented on and written about them and in many cases benefited from generous help and information freely given but rarely adequately acknowledged. He continues to lead a simple life of plain living guided by the aim of 'serving the people'.

Both his son Fufei and daughter Fuhui have been important in the development of the nursery. Chen Fuhui has been involved with all aspects, particularly propagation and seed storage and is currently the nursery manager. Many of the cultivar photographs in the book have been taken by her. Chen Fufei has organised the experimental cultivation of Gansu Mudan in different environments in Beijing.

knowledge of English and position as manager he sold abroad several thousands of small, medium and mature Gansu Mudan ordered from Peace Peony Nursery and kept all the money himself. When he left he took the nursery accounts and many of Chen Dezhong's mudan photographs, articles and letters. This episode in his career and the central role of Chen Dezhong in developing Gansu Mudan is glossed over in his own recent book on mudan.

Rows of seedling Gansu Mudan at the upper level of Peace Peony Nursery. In the distance is part of Lanzhou.

Grafted Gansu Mudan (mostly) being grown on.

Gansu Mudan where once there was barren earth; created from nothing using nothing but effort and passion and `the eye of faith'.

A significant strand in more ways than one in the story of Peace Peony Nursery is the involvement of Cheng Fangyun, initially an ambitious academic botanist at the Northwest Teaching University College at Lanzhao, now a professor at the Forestry University in Beijing and for a year in 1997 manager at the Nursery. While absorbing and building on Chen Dezhong's extensive knowledge of mudan he organised promotional literature which helped to make Peace Peony Nursery (and himself) better known. Using his

During the forty years of its development the importance of Peace Peony Nursery has been formally recognised in various ways. It has been part of the postgraduate distance-learning course run by the Horticultural Department of the Beijing Agricultural Institute. In 1993 it was designated by the China Forestry Department as one of the three largest plant resources nurseries in the whole country and has been designated as one of the model foundation nurseries for plants of China. Chen Dezhong has participated in research projects funded nationally and by the province of Gansu to investigate the ecological environment, altitude and biological properties of the natural distribution areas of wild Mudan. The nursery is regarded as the Demonstration Base for Production of Ziban Mudan by the National Plants Association and the Forestry Ministry. It has also been designated a 'scenery and tourist' location by the Province, City and County, and recognised as such by the National Travel and Tourist Bureau. Every year the Peace Peony Nursery receives study tours organised

Mixed Gansu Mudan at Peace Peony Nursery.

Chen Fufei.

Chen Fuhui.

by universities and colleges of higher education and visits by students on the training courses organised by the provincial administration and has become a base for collective research, production and education from outside the province. More recently it has received visits from horticultural experts from many countries and is now an essential part of the itinerary of peony tours from Europe and the United States.

Over 500 varieties of Gansu Mudan cultivated in the Nursery have obtained National Patents,

International PCT patents as well as patents from the National Forestry Ministry. Peace Peony Nursery varieties are praised and admired by mudan specialists, scholars and enthusiasts worldwide although these admirers are often unaware of the origins of the plants. The range of colours and flower forms introduced is enormous, and easily overlooked now that seed from the plants developed initially at Peace Peony Nursery is collected and sown elsewhere to produce equally spectacular plants. The varieties with large blotches on the back is a development

Mixed Gansu Mudan at Peace Peony Nursery. Here, as at Phedar Nursery and at La Pivoine Bleue the guiding spirit is indulgence in the plants. Carefully controlled, regimented planting is considered, but never happens.

that deserves special mention. Seedlings, mature plants and grafted specimens have been exported to North America, Australasia, Japan and Europe. Particularly pleasing for Chen Dezhong is the widespread use of his plants in other parts of China such as the North-East Provinces, Inner Mongolia, Tibet, Henan, Shanghai, Beijing, Shandong, Xinjiang and Wuhan. Almost all the Gansu Mudan now increasingly widely cultivated in gardens and nurseries in China and other countries have originated directly or indirectly in Peace Peony Nursery.

His own research outcome – the Near-Origin Integration Method Used in the Cultivation of Ziban (purple-blotched) Mudan – won a patent certificate from the State Patent Bureau of China in October 1995. In May the following year it was also certified as an international patent (PCT/CN96).

Peace Peony Nursery is situated in the Peace Economic Development Zone in Yuzhong County south-east of Lanzhou. It is now close to a motorway and about 10km from the city centre, 15 km from Lanzhou Railway Station and 90 km by motorway from Zhongchuan (Lanzhou) Airport. It is located in a branch of the Xinlong Mountains Range where it is said `three mountains gather and two dragons meet´.

From 7 hectares of barren land initially, Peace Peony Nursery has gradually reclaimed more of the adjacent hillsides. There are now about 70 hectares under various degrees of cultivation, about two-thirds of which is devoted to mudan and one third to trees for greening bare land. There is a ten hectare display nursery with over seven hundred mudan varieties and two hectares where all the wild species are grown. The future development is not entirely clear. The nursery has always been a part of the local community and parts of the cultivated land have been used for local economic development. Another area is now a cemetery which, ironically, provides significant income. The city, county and provincial management have plans to further expand the nursery as a more formally arranged mudan exhibition garden and general arboretum as a visitor and tourist attraction and as a 'dragon enterprise' in mudan cultivation. There are also plans to expand the experimental side of the nursery's activities in other locations with very different environmental conditions. This development would support the 'Maxian Mountain High and Cold Mudan Nursery' and 'Jinshixia Dry Land Mudan Nursery', with a combined area of over 240 hectares, that Chen Dezhong began to establish in 2002. As these two sites become productive there will be mudan in flower from the late April into July and the objective will be to produce and select new varieties of Mudan even more adaptable to cold and to dry weather and even more versatile in their usages and which extend the flowering season. Chen Fuhui will probably manage the restructured Peace Peony Nursery and Chen Fufei may move from the experimental nursery at Beijing to manage the other sites. Chen Dezhong is also working on another project, a study of medicinal uses of wild plants readily available.

The nursery soil is a very deep loess loam, pH 8.1 that drains quite well and cracks as it dries into lumps which crumble easily and evenly into very fine dust. All plants, seedlings and grafts, are grown directly in open soil. Altitude is 1780m, annual rainfall is 35cm, mostly in Spring and Autumn. The seasons, in the continental climate, are predictable, with frost or snow rare after the end of the long, severe winters. Spring and autumn are short and there are only about 155 frost free days. Extreme temperatures are 35 and 25ºC. The corresponding numbers for the trial nursery at Beijing are 50m, 50cm, 190 and 40 and 14ºC.

8.2 Phedar Research and Experimental Nursery

Phedar Nursery was effectively established in 1986 by the acquisition of its present site, an awkward, sloping bit of land near Stockport 13 km south-east of Manchester in sight of the Pennine hills. About half of the 1.5 hectares is terraced for intensive cultivation, the other half is too steep and dark but provides interesting inauspicious situations for trial growing of plants. The specialities are helleborus species and herbaceous paeonia species . The aim of the nursery is to examine taxonomic problems and horticultural questions by growing only authentic

Will McLewin

Eric Stead

Hu Xiaoling

wild-collected examples of different species in the same conditions and to make reliably named and identified plants availale. Few plants are grown simply for sale but usually plants surplus to study requirements are available. It also specialises in Gansu Group peonies and mudan species.

The work on helleborus species is based on over 17 years visiting the Balkans for fieldwork before, during and since the troubles in former Jugoslavia. Over 300 wild locations have been involved in observing and collecting specimens and seed. The taxonomy of acaulescent hellebores is particularly problematic and Phedar Nursery is recognised in many countries as a unique source of information and insight and for shedding light on the problems if not yet always on solutions. Many botanic gardens and hellebore students and enthusiasts have contacted or visited the nursery to obtain reliably named species plants.

A excellent Gansu Mudan at Phedar Nursery: not *Paeonia rockii* and not `Rock's Peony`, not even, strictly a `P. rockii hybrid`. In fact, an unnamed seedling. It could be named but doing so would not make any difference to the plant or to the esteem in which it is held.

Margaret Walty at Phedar Nursery in pursuit of He Ping Er Qiao and other Gansu Mudan.

Gansu Mudan at Phedar Nursery.

such things. Phedar Nursery's involvement, latterly an obsession, with Gansu Mudan began with the conviction that most of what was said about *P. rockii* and 'Rock's peony' was inaccurate and that there were many similar or associated plants that should be better known and more widely available. Once involved with Gansu Mudan the plants themselves took over, leading to arrangements with Peace Peony Nursery and La Pivoine Bleue Nursery and to a passionate enthusiasm that shows no signs of abating.

With peonies the approach has been different because such sustained fieldwork has not been practicable. Visits to Italy, Balkan countries, Russia, Georgia and China have helped to build a network of botanists to collect wild seed. The cause of growing, studying and enjoying true examples of species peonies has been served by making the results of their combined efforts widely available to peony enthusiasts who care about

Accuracy of nomenclature remains a guiding principle of Phedar Nursery. It is fuelled by the apparent indifference to such matters by almost all media commentators, sustained by a willingness to live with nomenclature problems until sufficient first-hand evidence has been accumulated, and demonstrated by open and explicit comments and guidance in all the literature and lists they produce.

Will McLewin was a mathematics lecturer at Manchester University for 27 years before leaving to work full-time with plants. He is, or more precisely was, an accomplished alpinist, the first British mountaineer to climb all the 4000metre peaks of the Alps without guides, many solo. He continues to struggle to play the French horn, nowadays only in chamber music. The nursery would probably not have survived, certainly not have flourished, without the help and advice of Eric Stead, a biologist and friend who also has cheerfully succumbed to the splendours of Gansu Mudan. Another vital source of help and advice, particularly with contacts and all matters Chinese is the academic linguist and lecturer Dr Hu Xiaoling. Her main research area is the historical development of the Chinese language but recently she too has developed expertise in and enthusiasm for Gansu Mudan.

The soil at Phedar Nursery, mostly about pH 6.5, is a shallow woodland loam over very heavy clay or rocky shale. The seasons are ill-defined and the overall climate pleasant and moderate but very unpredictable and quite often wet. Winters are mostly fairly mild, usually with short cold periods and some unseasonal warm spells. Of the average 38 days with air frost some quite late in Spring are usual but rarely prolonged. Average extreme temperatures are -6 and 30ºC, although -12 and 33ºC have been recorded. The average through the year of hours of sunshine is 3.8 per day. The average annual rainfall of 90cm can come as sustained heavy rain or even more sustained fine drizzle. Recent Springs have been unhelpfully dry and summer weather can be almost anything.

8.3 La Pivoine Bleue

A passion for peonies of all kinds precipitated Robert and Nicole Pardo's change from dealing

Robert Pardo and Will McLewin at Courson Plant Fair.

er. By exhibiting at major plant fairs like those at Courson their medal winning displays of peonies have helped to make Gansu Mudan and the wild species better known. All their plants, peonies

Nicole Pardo and Will McLewin at Courson Plant Fair.

in fine art to running their increasingly influential specialist plant nursery in SW France. La Pivoine Bleue was established in 1995 near Auch in the Gers region of Gascony in sight of the eastern Pyrenees mountains. Since then the range of peonies they grow and propagate has steadily increased and includes new herbaceous varieties originating in France to complement the many more traditional varieties. Following the establishment of cooperative links with Peace Peony Nursery and Phedar Nursery, Chinese peonies, especially Gansu Mudan, both grafted and from seed, are now the main focus of their work. However all peonies, woody, intersectional or herbaceous, and particularly the true wild species, are welcome inhabitants at La Pivoine Bleue, partly to be grown experimentally and partly to be made available when possible. They are ably assisted in all the nursery activities by Coralie Christiani, particularly with recording and photographing new plants as they develop and flow-

Coralie Christiani and Robert Pardo at La Pivoine Bleue Nursery.

and a range of unusual bulbs and perennials many from wild seed, are grown outside, some in open ground, some in raised beds or enormous tubs of prepared soil. This approach, like that at Peace and Phedar nurseries ensures strong plants that will grow on well and contributes to demonstrating the versatility (and the splendours) of Gansu Mudan.

The soil, pH 6.5, is a heavy clay that supports mudan well once they are established although the natural drainage is barely adequate. They have basically a Mediterranean climate with mild winters (unlike those of Gansu). The annual rainfall of 12cm is barely sufficient and although it comes mostly when it is needed in Spring and Autumn the hot and dry Summers are sometimes fierce enough to induce early dormancy in the mudan plants. The temperature is normally in the range 7 to 17ºC but up to 35º can be expected in Summer and -14º has been recorded in Winter.

Margaret Walty at Phedar Nursery.

Nursery Contact Details

Peace Peony Nursery:
Chen Fuhui
e-mail: chenfuhui1@hotmail.com

Phedar Research and Experimental Nursery:
Will McLewin
Address: Phedar Research and Experimental Nursery
42 Bunkers Hill, Romiley, Stockport, U.K. SK6 3DS
Telephone and Fax: (0044) (0) 161 430 3772
e-mail: mclewin@phedar.com
www.phedar.com

La Pivoine Bleue:
Robert and Nicole Pardo
Address: La Pivoine Bleue, A Sechan Dessus, 32550 Montegut, France
Telephone and Fax: (0033) (0) 5 62 65 63 56
e-mail: pivoine.bleue@free.fr
www.pivoine-bleue.com

Paeonia Gansu Group 'Li Chun'

丽
春

SECTION 3

GANSU MUDAN CULTIVARS

---

9. CULTIVAR CLASSIFICATION AND CULTIVAR NAMES

9.1 Classification of cultivars and classification characters

It seems to us helpful to arrange the cultivars illustrated into categories in terms of flower colour and flower form. This gives a basic structure to the list overall and makes comparisons, and possibly finding alternatives, easier. It also demonstrates more clearly the relatively small differences between basically similar varieties. Any characteristic is manifested in practice essentially as a continuum so that when discreet categories are chosen there are many intermediate or ambiguous examples. A few minutes spent arranging cultivars into a usefully small number of recognised colour and form categories is enough to show that it cannot be done entirely consistently. So this arrangement should not be taken very seriously.

Also classification of varieties should not be confused with specification of individual varieties. Specification entails description of many morphological and horticultural characters: flower colour or colours and flowering period; flower form including petals, stamens (anthers and filaments); carpels (stigma, follicles and seed); leaves (overall structure and individual leaflet shape, colour at various times); growth (upright or spreading, few or many twigs and branches, slow or vigorous); ecological uses and environmental tolerances. Other characters may be significant, hairs on leaves or leaf veins, stickiness of various parts, and so on.

It is possible with peonies, especially with Gansu Mudan to produce 'spurious precision': a detailed description of a plant that it frequently does not wholly comply with. In many cultivars the flower colour changes during the life of the flower, opening pink and becoming white for example. For the more complex or more developed forms the appearance of the flower and the impression it gives change considerably as it opens and expands. Young plants often display variation in many characters, particularly flower form but also flower colour, both from year to year and between individual flowers. For some varieties where we have suitable photographic evidence there are two or more pictures but this is to draw attention to this possibility not to these particular plants. Also flower characters may change noticeably when a plant is moved to a different environment. This character trait of mudan is both important to emphasise and difficult to put in perspective. Perhaps it is best summarised by saying that in normal circumstances (whatever that might mean) mudan can be expected to grow and appear as pictured but that variations should not come as a great surprise and may be transient. For Gansu Mudan there is the further considerable complication of the basal blotches on the petals. They vary in shape and size and colour and form from variety to variety and can also vary in appearance from year to year.

Partly for these reasons we have not attempted to provide detailed prose specifications for cultivars. The classification by colour and form gives basic information and the pictures give a lot more that does not need to be repeated in words. For varieties that have been observed to flower noticeably earlier or later than most or grow noticeably more upright or more spreading than most or are more vigorous this is indicated in the main list of pinyin names 11.1.

1) Classification by colours

The almost traditional classification of mudan flower colours in China is white, yellow, green, pink, red, purple, black, blue and blended. The way these labels are assigned needs some explanation. White is not as simple as it may seem. It has to include white with a very faint trace of blue or pink but where the tinge of another colour pervades much of the flower it is put with that other colour, or with blended. There are no true yellow Gansu Mudan (so far) but a few cultivars look at least cream, especially when placed beside clear white flowers, and these are classified as yellow. Similarly there are no really green flowers, just a few with green tips or which look particularly green as they open before turning white. Pink poses severe problems. When does dark pink become red or purple and when does faintly bluish pink become blue? In China red is used more freely, for flowers which have shades of other colours, and particularly for dark pink. There are actually very few mudan which are clearly a true red. And think how many names there are in English for different reds or near reds. Purple, when applied to mudan, is very rarely the true 'royal purple'. Instead it is used for 'bluish reds or pinks'. There are no truly blue mudan, although some recent cultivars are impressively close. Most so-called blue mudan are bluish-pink, or pinkish-blue. Some might be called mauve if that word could be used without its pejorative implication. Black, here as elsewhere, means

simply 'very dark' and even then it really means 'relatively dark'. Blended is used for flowers that are clearly a mixture of two (or more) colours apart from the dark blotch and sometimes this is clearly the case. But the blotches complicate things greatly. Almost always the edge of a black blotch will be purple or crimson and sometimes the blotch appears to bleed out into the main part of the petal to give a bicolour effect. We have opted to classify red, purple and blue fairly consistently and distinct from pink. Consequently pink includes wide colour variation.

The classification into colours here is an uncomfortable compromise between Chinese and Western conventions that is meant to be fairly consistent and helpful rather than definitive. Exactly the same applies to the grouping of varieties into different flower forms.

2) Classification by flower forms

The development of complex flower forms is a phenomenon of cultivation. In general mutations of flowers from the simple form with an open bowl of petals and normal male and female parts are less fertile and less likely to be fertilised and so when they occur in the wild they do not persist. In cultivation abnormal mutations are actively sought and propagated. Gansu Mudan do not have the long and intensive history of cultivation and directed breeding of Central Plains hybrid. Consequently the range of flower forms is not so extensive so a smaller list of flower forms than that described in, for example, `Chinese Tree Peony,´ (see chapter 2, p. 24) is adequate.

The development from the 'single' flower form of the wild species happens in three ways. There can be extra petals, more-or-less the same shape, either simply some extra petals to the normal ten or extra complete whorls of petals. The stamens can become petaloid, to a greatly variable extent. The carpels can become petaloid, again in a variety of ways. As with flower colour any categorisation into different forms involves compromises and there are ambiguous varieties. The possibility for more complex or more developed flowers seems to be an inherent character of mudan and it is not particularly unusual for plants in cultivation to produce more complex flowers when they become well established and are growing strongly. Different flower forms can sometimes occur on the same plant or the same branch or from year to year. Even true wild plants of P. rockii have occasionally been seen to exhibit some degree of doubling in flowers when grown in favourable conditions in cultivation.

The names given to the more traditional different mudan flower forms are names of other genera, which is both irritating and unhelpful. To say a mudan flower has rose form is no more useful than saying a certain rose has mudan form. However this is simply a question of convention and is separate from three other complications. There is no name so far for single flowers with just a few narrowly petaloid stamens among the normal stamens. This is presumably regarded as an aberrant transient form intermediate between single and some form of double. There are some flowers which have what is called proliferate form. When analysed closely they appear to have one flower imposed in the centre of another almost complete flower - two sets of petals separated by and separating two sets of stamens but only one set of carpels. Proliferation is totally different to fasciation, where two or more flowers are fused together side by side. Proliferation can occur with most double forms but in most cases this complex structure is not obvious. There is also an intermediate double form called 'golden circle' with the central petals, apparently petaloid stamens, still surrounded by a ring of normal or narrowly petaloid stamens. Here, these three forms of flower development and yet more subdivisions are subsumed in the more common traditional forms. There is a much more detailed discussion of flower form in `*Chinese Tree Peony*' in the context of the Central Plains (suffruticosa) Group.

(1) Single form: 2 whorls of normal, wide, large and fairly flat petals; stamens and carpels usually normal, rarely abnormal; fertile. Some varieties with a few narrowly petaloid stamens are included in this form.

(2) Lotus form: 3-4 whorls of normal wide and large petals, neatly arranged; stamens and carpels usually normal, rarely abnormal; fertile.

(3) Rose form: more than 4 whorls of normal petals that are wide and neat, large but be-coming smaller from the outside towards the centre; and stamens usually reduced in number and sometimes some petaloid, carpels usually slightly petaloid; usually fertile. Here this group has been extended to include the similar but slightly less developed form called chrysanthemum and some proliferate varieties.

(4) Anemone form: 2 outer whorls of wide, large and neat petals; stamens are mostly or entirely petaloid, mostly narrow, sometimes with anthers on the tips of these petals; carpels normal or reduced and petaloid; occasionally proliferate; usually fertile.

(5) Crown form: 2-5 outer whorls of normal petals; stamens completely or almost completely variously petaloid, sometimes some still with anthers; carpels largely or completely petaloid; the inner petals raised to form a crown shape; usually not fertile.

(6) Globular form: stamens are completely petaloid and resembling normal petals; carpels petaloid or absent; outer petals sometimes reflexed; overall shape round or even oval; not fertile.

3) Classification by blotches

For the simpler flower forms where the blotches are clearly visible a further stage of classification is possible, using the descriptions of blotches needed for more detailed cultivar specification. The seven colours of the blotches are light red, dark red, brownish red, bluish, purple, black and blended. Blotches are frequently blended in the sense of having a different coloured edge. There are various blotch shapes, including round, ovoid, elliptical, rhomboid, triangular, open V-shape. Then there is the question of solid or hollow blotch, there is the nature of the edge of the blotch from neat and precise to feathery or bleeding out and the size of the blotch either absolute or relative to the petal size. And then there are the back blotches. Thankfully the pictures can speak for themselves on most of these details, except to make the point that while the blotches are mostly obscured in some of the more developed double forms, when the petals fall they are spectacularly revealed, and resemble the plucked feathers of an exotic bird.

It is important to point out that the blotches, like the flower form, can in some cases vary from year to year and tend to be larger when the plant is flourishing. There is some evidence to suggest that this effect is greater with back blotches.

Additional information is given in the main cultivar list 11.1. We emphasise again that classification into colour and form categories is in many individual cases debateable and is intended to be helpful rather than taken very seriously.

9.2 Cultivar Names

Gansu Mudan names have three parts:

1. The actual given name in Chinese Characters.

2. The name in *pinyin*. This is the name that should be used as a name 'in English'.

3. A version of the name in English to convey the approximate meaning.

The translation of plant names from one language to another is often problematic because the name may have cultural implications beyond the words themselves. The collection of Chen Dezhong and Chen Fuhui's names for Gansu Mudan cultivars is an impressive achievement in itself. Translation of their names into English involves two profound problems. The first concerns the great differences in the two languages. The second comes from the poetic or allusive or idiomatic nature of many of the names.

To begin with the two languages: just as in English, individual Chinese words/characters often have multiple meanings or at least multiple interpretations that depend on the context in which they are used. (Strictly the terms 'word' and '(Chinese) character' do not mean the same but here we can gloss over the difference and regard them as interchangeable.) For example, jade is used to mean more than simply the semi-precious stone that is carved for ornaments. The character for jade is used to signify value or

beauty. More bizarrely when used adjectivally, it has unpredictable implications. A particular case is the phrase 'jade building' which does not necessarily signify a luxurious or magnificent building but one where (historically) young girls live. Consequently particular noun characters need to be translated differently according to the context and apparently inconsistently. Another very significant difference is that noun characters do not have plural forms and verb characters do not conjugate. So 'zhu' can mean pearl or pearls and 'peng' can mean hold or holds or holding or held. In prose passages, the particular meaning may simply be implied or may be indicated by characters preceding or following, but such characters are absent in the plant names.

The names of Gansu Mudan themselves are in many cases more complicated than Western plant names. They have a poetic quality that is rare in Western plant names and they draw on a very wide range of images. While other groups of cultivar names will include references to animals we doubt that camels will make an appearance elsewhere. Frequently more than one image or idea is involved but because definite and indefinite articles ('the' and 'a/an') are absent in the plant names, and prepositions like 'on' and 'of' and 'with' and conjunctions such as 'and' are mostly absent, the most appropriate English equivalent is not obvious. (The absence of definite and indefinite articles applies to the Chinese language as a whole, not just to plant names. There is no definite article and a character equivalent to the indefinite article is used very rarely.) There are a few names with characters from stories and only very occasionally names of individuals, friends, etc. There are no consciously clever or smart names and the ubiquitous practice of choosing 'enticing' names to encourage sales is entirely absent. Some plant names are well-known Chinese idioms. In contrast with broadly similar western idioms or sayings the meaning is often not obvious and not accurately translatable in less than a paragraph. Many consist of four characters/syllables and this colloquial feature has clearly influenced many of the names given to Gansu Mudan cultivars. For names which are idioms more or less well known in China we have mostly not tried to replace them with alternative names which have similar meanings in English. Instead, for such names and for names that evoke events in stories, ancient or modern, we have indicated this in the main cultivar list, 11.1, provided an approximate literal translation and added a comment in 11.2 outlining the background context.

It is important to appreciate that the names that should be used for cultivars are the pinyin names. The English equivalents in 11.1 are provided to explain the meaning of the Chinese name but are not intended as replacement names in English and should not be used as such. The *pinyin* names themselves are ambiguous because each word in *pinyin* represents several Chinese characters. For example, the *pinyin* word 'hong' can mean 'red' or 'rainbow' or 'huge'. Some particular meanings can be identified when the pronunciation tone is indicated but one *pinyin* word with one particular tone may have several distinctive meanings. Clearly one can guess that some meanings are inappropriate in the context of flower names. Such problems are of course not unique to Chinese and have to be faced in any translation process. But when what is being translated is groups of three or four characters forming the name such problems are particularly acute. In providing English equivalents we have tried wherever possible to give the simplest and most direct meaning while retaining something of the Chinese character. In a few examples where the simplest literal English equivalent has an idiomatic implication, pejorative for example, unintended in the Chinese name we have been a little more imaginative.

Most of the Chinese names are chosen to convey a fairly complex or poetic vision with three or four characters which when spoken are pleasingly euphonious. A detailed analysis of the whole collection of names would be an interesting exercise in itself but is inappropriate here. However it is insightful to outline several types of names which occur fairly frequently. One consists of two distinctive ideas, typically two nouns with adjectives or other modifiers. As an example, 'Bin Shan Xue Lian' is literally 'ice mountain snow lotus' and in most cases we have not changed the English equivalent

from this simplest form. But there are several other versions which are equally valid such as 'ice mountains snow lotuses' or 'icy mountain snowy lotus' or 'snow lotus of ice mountain' or 'icy mountain with snow lotus' and so on. A similar category is one noun with two adjectives or modifiers. A third category where the most appropriate equivalent is less clear consists of names that involve a verb character, for example 'Hong Lou Cang Jin'. The literal equivalent is 'red building hide gold' which is prosaic and inelegant. The two obvious alternatives are 'red building hides gold' and 'red building hiding gold' one or other of which we have in general preferred. There are slightly more inventive and equally valid possibilities such as 'gold hidden in red buildings' and we note in passing that the two characters for 'red building' actually denote a building or part of a building where, in earlier times, the young girls of a prosperous extended family would live and the 'hidden gold' would actually refer to the young girls and not actual gold pieces. Names with two verb characters are even more problematic. In a fourth category are names which are Chinese idioms where the literal equivalent is largely meaningless or quite unlike the understood meaning. An example is the four characters of 'Qian Zi Bai Tai'. The characters for Qian and Bai are those for thousand and hundred and Zi Tai means posture. This phrase to a Chinese person conveys the idea that in a large assemblage of basically similar objects each one does have an individual character so this phrase could be said of clouds in the sky or flowers at the market or a range of mountains but more debatably of the famous terracotta warriors at Xian. A fifth category that cannot meaningfully be translated simply has names that are phrases invoking scenes or characters or events from Chinese legends, both ancient and relatively recent. A splendid example is 'Yu Lu Lian Dan', literally 'jade stove make immortality pills'. This is one of several Gansu Mudan names which come from very famous and fantastical sixteenth century story 'Xi You Ji' (Journey to the West) in which the Monkey King (Wu Kong) steals and eats the magic pills that the Emperor in Heaven had ordered to be made in the Jade Stove to make him immortal.

Particular *pinyin* words (corresponding to particular Chinese characters) that occur frequently with an implied meaning beyond the literal meaning include:

'Yu'. This word appears in over 60 names. Literally it means jade but in a poetic or imaginative sense it is used adjectivally to mean something valuable or special or beautiful. So 'Yu Pan' is literally jade plate and in 'Yu Pan Fen Zhu' jade plate is what is meant, but in 'Yu Lou Cang Jiao', literally 'jade building hide lady', the building is not made of jade nor even necessarily has the colour of jade but 'Yu Lou' is the part of a house where the unmarried girls would live. Note that jade itself can be green or white and is also used as a girl's name.

'He' and 'Lian' both meaning lotus are sometimes used as part of a flower name even when the cultivar does not have lotus form.

'Jin' meaning gold is used rather like Yu (jade) to signify something valuable or splendid or special or strong and is often used in conjunction with other colours. It is used both as a noun and as an adjective, much as gold is used in English in fact. So in 'Yu Guan Jin Zhu', literally 'jade crown gold pearl', 'gold' means neither the metal nor the colour but signifies 'splendid' or 'magnificent' (the same is true with 'jade' in this example). In 'Jin Cheng Wan Xia', the character for 'gold' when combined with 'Cheng' (city) indicates 'impregnable fortress'.

The literal meaning of 'lou' is 'building' but in the context of plant names the building is rarely a simple house so we have usually translated this word as 'pavilion'. In many cases, the other characters in the name imply a building with some special significance, typically containing something precious and, yet again, often the building where the young girls of an extended (and prestigious) family live.

'Xian' literally meaning 'thread' appears in several names. When it is with the noun 'nu'

(woman or lady) the implication is that the lady is weaving, so 'Zi Xian Nu' means 'a woman weaving with purple thread'. As there is no English word meaning 'female weaver' we have chosen the simple equivalent of 'thread lady'.

One name that perhaps deserves some detailed comment is 'Shu Sheng Peng Mo', if only because it has become a fashionable name that is used (usually incorrectly) for any single white flower with a strong blotch. The usual translation is 'scholar holding ink' but 'Shu Sheng Peng Mo' is far from simple. 'Shu' signifies 'to write' or 'book' and in conjunction with other characters signifies various sorts of written or printed documents both personal and official. 'Sheng' indicates aspects of life including 'birth'. 'Shu Sheng' together is somewhat archaic expression meaning more a student or bookworm or pedant than a scholar in the modern sense of the word which implies a level of distinction or achievement. 'Peng' and 'Mo' mean literally 'to hold' and 'ink' but when used with 'Shu Sheng', 'Mo' means not literally 'ink, in a bottle' but the (usually black) stone with a saucer-like hollow in which a student would put water and then grind in the hollow with another stone called an ink stick. So 'Shu Sheng Peng Mo' could be translated 'Bookworms hold inkstones'.

In many of the names of Gansu Mudan there are characters/pinyin words that appear in other names, indeed the whole of some names appear as part of another name. This should be regarded as simply coincidence. It does not imply a 'parental' connection between plants or a connection as part of a 'breeding programmme' or a 'strain' or even a basic similarity. Each name should be regarded as an independent entity. Also, while some names are descriptive of the flower most are not, and even colours appearing as part of the name are not necessarily accurately indicative of the actual flower colour.

9.3 The use of mudan cultivar names in practice.
Ideally, perhaps, a named mudan cultivar would be propagated vegetatively so that all plants bearing the name are genetically identical and

hence are botanically/morphologically identical and have the same basic form and cultural requirements. The term 'cultivar' is neither synonymous with nor equivalent to 'variety' but effectively supersedes and replaces it. A cultivar can be a clone but the concept explicitly covers assemblages of plants which are very similar (overall or in a particular aspect). In practice, while Gansu Mudan are grafted quite extensively they are also widely grown from seed and 'identified' when they flower. Subsequent vegetative propagation of such plants complicates the situation. This tradition, by no means confined to Chinese horticulture, of regarding similar looking plants as equivalent or interchangeable, results in variation among mudan labelled with the same name. The recently introduced concept of a 'cultivar group' in a sense codifies and condones the practice. Of course the questions of context and degree are critically important. To some extent the practice is not unreasonable and much of the time it is inconsequential. There seems little doubt that it is widespread in China and on the whole tolerated there although this is not said in its defence. Consequently the cultivar names should to some extent be regarded as names for types, or even as the names of cultivar groups. There are, of course, particular plants to which the cultivar name was given, and clones of them which absolutely correctly carry that name. However in many cases, particularly with the more popular or more common cultivars, plants will have been labelled with a name when they are not clones of the original but are only more-or-less similar. The problem of accuracy of cultivar names is no worse for paeonia than any other genus and there is a parallel problem with species plants. Labels with species names are attached to plants when in fact they are cultivated hybrids and have only a vague or merely presumed connection with the species in question.

There is a simple solution to this nomenclature problem. Unless there is precise and rigorous provenance to justify the name on the label a word such as 'type' should be added. Thus Paeonia *xx* type would mean: this may be P. *xx*; or this looks more-or-less like what we believe P. *xx* looks like; or when we received this plant it was labelled P. *xx*; or P. *xx* has or may have been involved at some stage in the production of this plant; or this plant is, for horticultural purposes, equivalent in some sense, possibly even better than P. *xx*; or a mixture of all of these, but it is not possible to say with certainty that this is a true example of the plant to which the name P. *xx* was originally given. Such a designation, if widely adopted, would carry no derogatory implication. Quite the reverse, it would commend the integrity of the person responsible for the label. And it would be appropriate more often than not for plants in cultivation. Instead of 'type' the word 'group' could perhaps be used thus making explicit the implications of this relatively recent concept.

Returning to Gansu Mudan, the many cultivars illustrated and the corresponding long lists of names underlines the approach of the nurseries featured in Chapter 6, and of Peace Peony Nursery in particular. From a commercial or even simply practical point of view there are too many names and in some cases differences are not greatly significant. However the main motivation of all three nurseries is the development and testing of the Paeonia Gansu Group as a whole and all such plants that arise are regarded with affection. Bearing in mind that there are four basic variable morphological characters, the flower colour, the flower form, the blotch colour and form and the natural growth form of the plant there will undoubtedly be many more distinct cultivars named. The illustrations here of as yet unnamed plants and the present absence of strong yellows and some character combinations make this clear. In fact of the plants that have been named at Peace Peony Nursery less than two thirds are illustrated and listed here. Intensive commercial exploitation of Gansu Mudan has already begun in other places exploiting, quite rightly the vigour, versatility and outstanding ornamental value of the plants: building on if seldom acknowledging Chen Dezhong's achievement.

10.   GANSU MUDAN CULTIVAR PICTURES,
arranged by colour and form

The classification categories of 9.1 lead to a natural ordering and a corresponding reference number for each cultivar that locates each in the sequence of pictures.

Colour	Form
1. white	1. single
2. yellow	2. lotus
3. green	3. rose
4. pink	4. anemone
5. red	5. crown
6. purple	6. globular
7. black	
8. blue	
9. blended/mixed	

Within each of the nine colours, beginning with white, cultivars are grouped in the six form categories, beginning with single. Thus 1.3.10 Bei Ji Hu is the tenth cultivar with rose form and white colour and 4.6.18 He Ping Lian is the eighteenth cultivar with globular form and pink colour.

Cultivars are placed in numerical order apart from small displacements to accommodate pictures of different sizes.

In addition to the named cultivars, in each category a selection of unnamed plants that are still 'on trial' are illustrated. These are numbered only, for example 1.3#2 and 4.6#3, and not referred to elsewhere.

For a few cultivars there are two to four pictures as examples to show significantly different looking flowers on the same plant.

1.1.19 Xiong Mao

1.1#6

1.1.11 Yin Pan Zi Zhu

1.1.31 Pan Pan

1.1.1 Bing Shan Xue Lian

1.1.19 Xiong Mao

1.1.46 Da Mo Gu Ya

1.1#3

1.1#4

1.1#5

1.1#8

1.1.10 Xue Hai Chen Guang

1.1.51 Hong Zong Lie Ma

1.1#9

1.1.57 Guan Ai

1.1#7

1.1#10

1.1.56 Zong Ban Bai

1.1#11

1.1.6 Da Xue Hai Bing Xin

1.1#12

1.1#14

1.1#15

1.1#16

1.1#17

1.1#18

1.1.43 Fo Guang Fen

1.1#19

1.1#20

1.1#21

1.1#1

1.1#2

1.1#13

1.1#38

1.1#22

1.1#23

1.1#24

1.1.24 Xue Hai Dan Xin

1.1.30 Yin Die Fei Wu

1.1.32 Mo Ban Yin Guang

1.1.45 Bei Dou Xing

1.1#25

1.1#26

1.1#27

1.1#29

1.1#30

1.1#31

1.1#32

1.1.54 Jin Ye Bai

1.1.47 Ao Yun Zhi Guang

1.1#34

1.1#35

1.1#36

1.1#37

1.1#39

1.1#40

1.1#41

1.1#42

1.1#43

1.1#44

1.1#45

1.1#46

1.1#47

1.1#48

1.1#49

1.1#50

1.1#51

1.1.2 Shu Sheng Peng Mo

1.1.3 Bai Bi Lan Xia

1.1.4 Hei Fa Nu Lang

1.1.5 Xue Hai Bing Xin

1.1.7 Yu Feng Dian Tou

1.1.8 Bai He Liang Chi

1.1.9 Wu Fa Lan Dai

1.1.12 Ju He San Bian

1.1.13 Mu Chun Bai

1.1.14 Hei Long Tan

1.1.15 Yi Dian Mo

1.1.16 Yi Ding Mo

1.1.17 Yu Long Bei

1.1.17 Yu Long Bei

1.1.18 Wu Kong Xiu Xing

1.1.19 Xiong Mao

1.1.20 Hei Bai Fen Ming

1.1.21 Zhong Xing Peng Yue

1.1.22 Bei Ji Xiong

1.1.23 Xue Hai Fang Xin

1.1.25 Xiao Bai Yu

1.1.26 Yan Huang Er Nu

1.1.27 Hei Fa Dan Xin

1.1.28 Wu Jiao Xing

1.1.31 Pan Pan

1.1.31 Pan Pan

1.1.33 Fu Ai

1.1.29 Yan Hua Chu Fang

1.1.34 Ai

1.1.35 Yin Pan Tuo Gui

1.1.36 Mei Ran Gong

1.1.37 Tong Xin Tong De

1.1.38 Cao Chuan Jie Jian

1.1.39 Bei Ji Guang

1.1.40 Xin Xing

1.1.41 Hong Xia Ying Xue

1.1.42 Tu Xing

1.1.43 Fo Guang Fen

1.1.44 Zhao Jun Fei Yun

1.1.48 Fen Die Chu Yu

1.1.49 Yu Shan Lun Jin

1.1.50 Xue Yu Zhi Huan

1.1.52 Ju Ban Fen

1.1.53 Jin Si Bai

1.2.16 Hong Guang Man Mian

1.1.55 Dian Jin Yan Wei Fen

1.1.57 Guan Ai

1.1.58 Xue Hua

1.2#1

1.2#2

1.2#5

1.2.7 Hong Fa Mo Nu

1.2.14 Yu Lu Lian Dan

1.2#6

1.2#7

1.2#8

1.2#9

1.2#10

1.2#11

1.2#12

1.2#13

1.2#14

1.2#15

1.2#16

1.2#17

1.2.14 Yu Lu Lian Dan

1.2.16 Hong Guang Man Mian

1.2#3

1.2#18

1.2.9 Xiu Fa Pi Jian

1.2.8 Yin Hai Hong Bo

1.2.2 Yin Yang Shan

1.2.3 Hong Chi Wei Bo

1.2.6 Re Xue Qing Chun

1.2.10 Qin Jin Zhi Hao

1.2.12 Qing Hai Hu Yin Bo

1.2.14 Yu Lu Lian Dan

1.2.1 Yao Tai Jiu Nu

1.2.13 Yuan Yang Pu

1.2.14 Yu Lu Lian Dan

1.2.15 Long Gong De Bao

1.3#2

1.3#3

1.3#4

1.2#4

1.2.11 Fen Lou Cha Cui

1.3.7 Lian Hua Shan

1.3.8 Yu Nu Tan Hai

1.3.10 Bei Ji Hu

1.2.4 Ji Gong

1.3.11 Xue Shan Yu Hui

1.3.12 Xue Zhan Chang Ban Po

1.2.5 Yu Tang Chun

1.3.12 Xue Zhan Chang Ban Po

1.3.14 Ba Jiao Shan

1.3.18 Fen Yu

1.3.19 Li Hua Zui Jiu

1.3.1 Gui Fu Ren

1.3.2 Fei Tian

1.3.3 Fen Mian Tao Sai

1.3.4 Xiao Xue

1.4#1

1.4#2

1.4#3

1.3.5 Xue Li Cang Jin

1.3.6 He Luo Yin Hai

1.3.8 Yu Nu Tan Hai

1.3.9 Yin Lou Hui Cai

1.4#4

1.4#5

1.4#6

1.3.13 Xue Shan Fei Hong

1.3.3 Fen Mian Tao Sai 1

1.3.15 Hong Ban Ju Hua Bai

1.3.16 Bing Shan Dian Yun

1.3.17 Bai Yi Da Xia

1.3.20 Yu Guan Cai Dai

1.4#7

1.4.1 Qi E Wo Bing

1.4.2 Xue Shan Jin Ding

1.4.6 Dian Jin Bai Yan Wei

1.4.6 Dian Jin Bai Yan Wei

1.4.2 Xue Shan Jin Ding

1.4.4 Zhen Zhu Bai

1.4.3 Xing Long Rui Xue

1.4.5 Jiao Yu

1.4.8 Jin Bo Dang Yang

1.4.10 Qi Lian Cai Hong

1.4.11 Fen Guan Jin Zhu

1.4.12 Ju Hua Fen

1.4.15 Yin Shan Dan Xia

1.4.7 Yan Wei Bai

1.4.7 Yan Wei Bai

1.4.7 Yan Wei Bai

1.4.9 Ju Hua Huang

1.5#2

1.5#3

1.5#4

1.4.11 Fen Guan Jin Zhu

1.4.12 Ju Hua Fen

1.4.13 Liu Yao Bai

1.4.14 Yu Lou Pi Cai

1.5.1 Yu Ban Xiu Qiu

1.5.4 Jiang Tai Gong Diao Yu

1.5.4 Jiang Tai Gong Diao Yu

1.5.2 Fen Bi Sheng Hui

1.5.6 Yu Guan Jin Zhu

1.5.7 Xing Yun

1.5.8 Tian Shan Ri Chu

1.5.9 Xing Guang Can Lan

1.5.10 Yu Lou Shan Jin

1.5.11 Feng Chu

1.5.27 Lan Hua Nu

1.5.13 Yu Guan Hei Fa

1.5.14 Yu Guan Lan Dai

1.5.16 Huo Fo Ju Shou

1.5.20 Long Yuan Xue

1.5.18 Huang He Lou

1.5.21 Yu Guan Xiang Cui

1.5.19 Ying Zhuang Su Guo

1.5.22 Xue Yuan Zao Chun

1.5.24 Bai Yi Nu Xia

1.5.14 Yu Guan Lan Dai

1.5#1

1.5.26 Xiao Lou Dian Yun

1.5.15 Xue Shan Wan Xia

1.5.27 Lan Hua Nu

1.5.4 Jiang Tai Gong Diao Yu

1.5.5 Jin Cheng Ming Yue

1.5.12 Jiao Mei

1.5.14 Yu Guan Lan Dai

1.6#1

1.6#2

1.6#3

1.5.3 Bai Zhang Bing

1.5.17 Yin Ju Cui Rui

1.5.23 Yu Lou Xiang Cui

1.5.25 Fen Ge Miao Jin

1.6#4

1.6#5

1.6.1 Xue Ye Han Yan

1.6.6 Bai Pao Jin Dai

1.6.3 Bei Guo Feng Guang

1.6.4 Xue Yuan Xin Huo

1.6.5 Yue Zhao Kun Lun

1.6.6 Bai Pao Jin Dai

1.6.6 Bai Pao Jin Dai

1.6.7 Wu Duo Jin Hua

1.6.11 Tian Gao Yun Dan

1.6.8 Kun Lun Qiu Se

1.6.9 Yin Bai He

1.6.10 Bai Yun Hong Xia

1.6.12 Gao Lou Cang Jiao

1.6.14 Bai Xiu Qiu

1.6.15 Yan Rao Bai Ta

1.6.13 Sai Bai He

1.6.14 Bai Xiu Qiu

1.6.2 Yu Lou Cang Jiao

2.1.2 Yin Si Bai

2.5.3 Bing Shan Cang Yu

2.5.2 Huang Yun

2.1.2 Yin Si Bai

2.1.5 Xiao Xue Hai Bing Xin

2.1.9 Huang Tu Goa Yuan

2.1.10 Huang Shan Chen Xi

2.1.3 Yu He Dian Yun

2.1.4 Pan Deng

2.1.6 Xue Hai Yin Zhen

2.1.1 Huang Lian

2.1.7 Hong Shu Lin

2.1.7 Hong Shu Lin

2.1.8 Huang He

2.3.1 Yu Guan Yue

2.3.2 Gao Yuan Shen Qiu

2.3.3 Wan Xue Ying Chun

2.4#1

2.4.1 Juan Bian Huang

2.5.1 Ju Hua Bai

2.6.1 Huang Jin Yu Zhui

3.1#1

3.1#2

3.1#3

3.4#1

3.5#1

3.5#2

3.5#3

3.5.3 Fen Yu Dian Cui

3.6#2

3.6#3

3.5.4 Bing Shang Fei Cui

3.5.1 Li Ren Zhuang

3.5.2 Jing Yu Dian Cui

3.6#1

3.1.1 Chun Dao Long Yuan

4.1.7 Lue Shi Fen Dai

4.1.12 Tie Mian Wu Si

4.1.1 Fen He

4.1.14 Gui Zhong Shao

4.1#2

4.1#3

4.1#4

4.1#5

4.1.4 Mo Chi Ying Yue

4.1.9 Fo Guang Hong

4.1#7

4.1#8

4.1#9

4.1.6 Xing Gao Cai Lie

4.1#11

4.1.10 Mo Chi Yan Xia

4.1#13

4.1.2 Fen Chi Ying Yue

4.1.3 Hong Hai Yin Zhou

4.1#13

4.1.5 Hong Lian

4.1#1

4.1.13 Jiao Yang

4.1.8 Ying Ri He Hua

4.1.12 Tie Mian Wu Si

4.1.12 Tie Mian Wu Si

4.2#2

4.2#3

4.2#5

4.1.11 Long Yuan Fen

4.1#10

4.1#12

4.2.1 Mo Nu

4.2.4 Hong Hai Yin Lang

4.2.3 Jiu Zhou Tai

4.2.8 Wan Hua Zi

4.2.5 Ne Zha Nao Hai

4.2.6 Er Long Xi Zhu

4.2.7 Wan Hua Hong

4.2#4

4.2#1

4.2.2 Xue Yuan Yu Hui

4.3#1

4.3#2

4.3#6

4.3#3

4.3#4

4.3#5

4.3.2 Fen Mo Deng Chang

4.3.3 Tan Hua Fen

4.3.4 Wen Jun Xin Meng

4.3.6 Da Qian Shi Jie

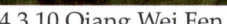

4.3.10 Qiang Wei Fen

4.3.5 Long Yuan Er Qiao

4.3.7 He Tang Qiu Bo

4.3.3 Tan Hua Fen

4.3.9 He Ping Fen

4.4#1

4.4#2

4.3.8 Jin Cheng Wan Xia

4.4.9 Qing Chun

4.4.1 Yu Lou Fen

4.4.4 Fen Guan Yu Dai

4.4.2 Qian Zi Bai Tai

4.4.5 Fen Yu San Tai

4.3.1 Fo Guang

4.4.7 Xue Shan Chui Yan

4.4.8 Hong Yi Nu Lang

4.4.3 Fen Guan Cai Die

4.4#3

4.4.10 Dai Yu Zang Hua

4.4.11 Zhen Zhu Nu

4.4.12 Zi Yun Feng

4.4.6 Zi Xia Dong Zhao

4.5.15 Ju Yuan Xin Xiu

4.5.20 Lan Xian Diao Jin Chan

4.4.5 Fen Yu San Tai

4.5.19 Qing Feng Wan Xia

4.5.26 Feng Guan Yu Zhu

4.5#1

4.5#2

4.5.1 Fen Yan Jiao

4.5.2 Xia Guang Wan Li

4.5.3 Xia Ran Qing Shan

4.5.5 Shen Nu

4.5.7 Chang E Shu Xiu

4.5.8 Xiao Xia

4.5.11 Zhong Jie Mei

4.5.12 Fen Lou Dan Xin

4.5.14 Jin Huan Fen

4.5.16 Hong Yun Shan

4.5.21 Fei Xiang Yu Zhou

4.5.17 Hong Xian Nu

4.5.17 Hong Xian Nu

4.5.18 Fen Yan Wei

4.5.18 Fen Yan Wei

4.5.22 Tia Mi De Meng

4.5.23 Li Fu Ren

4.5.6 Zi Xian Nu

4.5.9 Zui Fei

4.5.12 Fen Lou Dan Xin

4.5.24 Tao Yuan Ju Hui

4.5.13 Tao Hua Yuan

4.5.25 Hong Lou Dian Jin

4.5.4 Mu Yang Nu

4.5.10 Jiao Rong Chu Lu

4.5.17 Hong Xian Nu

4.5.27 He Ping Hong

4.5.28 Lan Guan Yu Dai

4.6#1

4.6#2

4.6#3

4.6#4

4.6.1 Chu E Zhan Chi

4.6.2 Lan Xian Nu

4.6.2 Lan Xian Nu

4.6.3 Li Xia Fen

4.6.4 Fen Guan Cai Dai

4.6.5 Shen Guang Yu Lu

4.6.8 Feng Zi Xiu Se

4.6.10 Yu Zhong Fen

4.6.12 Tian Shan Xia Nu

4.6.13 Fen Ge Piao Cai

4.6.14 Tao Hua Nu

4.6.16 Tao Hong Xiu Qiu

4.6.17 Jin Cheng Lan

4.6.20 Yin Xian Diao Jin Gui

4.6.22 He Ping Hong Xiu Qiu

4.6.23 Fen Yu Sheng Hui

4.6.24 Fei Yan Gui Chao

4.6.25 Zi Guan Yu Dai

4.6.2 Lan Xian Nu

4.6.11 Hong Lou Yu Ding

4.6.15 Zhong Shan Feng Yu

4.6.9 Lan Yue

4.6.19 Mai Ji Shan Yan Yun

4.6.16 Tao Hong Xiu Qiu

4.6.18 He Ping Lan

4.6.6 Feng Juan Can Yun

4.6.21 Diao Chan Bai Yue

4.6.4 Fen Guan Cai Dai

4.6.7 Chun Jiang Yan Bo

4.6.23 Fen Yu Sheng Hui

5.1.4 Xi Yang Hong

5.1#1

5.1#2

5.1#3

5.1#6

5.1#4

5.1#5

5.1#7

5.1#8

5.1#10

5.1.2 Hong Hai Jin Dao

5.1#9

5.1.5 Re Lie

5.1.6 Xi Qing You Yu

5.1.10 Xi Yue Bing Chuan

5.1.8 Shen Guang

5.1.3 Ju Yuan Shao Nu

5.1.1 Long Yuan Hong

5.1.7 Hong Qi Man Juan

5.1.3 Ju Yuan Shao Nu

5.1.9 Zi Jin Huan

5.2.3 Yan Li

5.2#4

5.2#5

5.2#3

5.2#6

5.3.1 Zi Ling Long

5.3#1

5.3.3 Zi Hai Yin Bo

5.3.4 Mo Guan Yu Zhu

5.4.1 Feng Xian

5.4.2 Zi Ta Dian Jin

5.3.2 Zi Yuan Yang

5.3.3 Zi Hai Yin Bo

5.5#1

5.5.1 Hong Lou Jin Chai

5.5.4 Zi Zhou Chou

5.5.3 Li Shi Mo Kui

5.5.5 Xuan Nu Gong

5.5.2 Chen Hong Yi Hai

5.5.5 Xuan Nu Gong

5.6#1

5.6.1 Hong Tai Yin Ge

6.1#9

6.1#12

6.1#7

6.1#14

6.1.5 Jin Cheng Nu Lang

6.1.5 Jin Cheng Nu Lang

6.1.5 Jin Cheng Nu Lang

6.1.8 Lan He

6.1#1

6.1#2

6.1#3

6.1.1 Shui Xing

6.1.8 Lan He

6.1.12 Lan Mo Shuang Hui

6.1.7 Bao Gong

6.1.4 Guang Hui Li Cheng

6.1.12 Lan Mo Shuang Hui

6.1.11 Juan Bian Lan He

6.1#4

6.1#5

6.1#6

6.1#8

6.1#10

6.1#11

6.1#13

6.1#15

6.1#17

6.1#18

6.1#19

6.1#20

6.1#21

6.1#22

6.1#23

6.1#24

6.1#26

6.1#27

6.1#28

6.1#29

6.1#30

6.1#31

6.1#32

6.1.2 You Yi

6.1.3 Hong Qian Niu

6.1.5 Jin Cheng Nu Lang

6.1.6 Zi Hai Yin Guang

6.1.5 Jin Cheng Nu Lang

6.1.7 Bao Gong

6.1.9 Nan Hai Jin Dao

6.1.9 Nan Hai Jin Dao

6.1.10 Bing Xin Lan He

6.1.12 Lan Mo Shuang Hui

6.2#1

6.2#2

6.2#3

6.2.3 Hong Hai Yin Bo

6.2#4

6.2.4 Zi Yan

6.2.3 Hong Hai Yin Bo

6.2#5

6.2.1 Mu Ai

6.2.2 Gao Gan Hong

6.2.1 Mu Ai

6.2.4 Zi Yan

6.2.5 Gu Cheng Xiang Hui

6.2.5 Gu Cheng Xiang Hui

6.3.4 Tao Hua Shan

6.3#1

6.3#2

6.3#3

6.3#4

6.3.2 Hong Hai Feng Yun

6.3.12 Lan Zhang Cai Wei

6.3.9 Jing Cheng Hong

6.3.6 Hong Zhen Zhu

6.3#5

6.3#6

6.3.1Huai Nian

6.3.3 Hong Hai Yang

6.3.4 Tao Hua Shan

6.3.5 Chun Man Ren Jian

6.3.7 Hong Yu Fan Lang

6.3.9 Jing Cheng Hong

6.3.10 Hong Yi Shao Nu

6.3.11 Xiu Lou Xiang Cui

6.3.13 Xiao Ban Lan Xiu Qiu

6.3.14 Zhou Mei Gui

6.3.16 Ri Mu Gui Tuo

6.3.17 Yi Jie Jin Lan

6.4#3

6.3.8 Tao Rong

6.3.18 Bao Shi Lan

6.3.9 Jing Cheng Hong

6.3.15 Chen Yuan Zi

6.4.3 Hong Guan Yin Xian

6.4.16 Zi Zhu Lin

6.4.26 Wu Yan Liu Se

6.4.17 Hong Lou Jing Meng

6.4#1

6.4#5

6.4.20 Zi Ta Xiang Cui

6.4.11 Nong Xia Man Tian

6.4.1 Jing Shen Huan Fa

6.4.12 Zi Pao Chen Shuang

6.4.2 Hong Lou Cang Jin

6.4.23 Geng Shang Yi Cen Lou

6.4.26 Wu Yan Liu Se

6.4.18 Zi Jin Guan

6.4.25 Lan Tian Meng

6.4#2

6.4#4

6.4#6

6.4.2 Hong Lou Cang Jin

6.4.4 Hong Hai Qing Long

6.4.5 Jin Yu Man Shan

6.4.8 Lan Yu San Cai

6.4.6 Chuan Jin Dai Yin

6.4.7 Hong Yun Tu Qi

6.4.8 Lan Yu San Cai

6.4.9 Hong Xia Man Tian

6.4.13 Zi Guan Yu Chi

6.4.10 Xiao Hong Ta

6.4.14 Ju Hua Zi

6.4.15 Zi Gui Yin Mai

6.4.19 Jin Huan Yin Xian

6.4.21 Zi Zhen Zhu

6.4.27 Lan Hai Yin Bo

6.4.24 Lan Hai Yin Lang

6.4.22 Ju Hua Lan

6.5#1

6.5.1 Tao Yuan Chun Se

6.5.4 Feng Cai

6.5.2 Man Tang Hong

6.5.9 Hong Zhou Chou

6.5.10 Yan Chun

6.5.11 Jiao Mei

6.5.12 Zi Guan Yu Zhu

6.5.17 Fu Li Hong

6.5.18 Zi Jin Ting

6.5.19 Zi Lou Cang Yu

6.5.20 Zi Lou Xiang Jin

6.5.21 Zi Pao Yin Bian

6.5.22 Zi Luo Yin Wei

6.5.23 Lan Xing Shan Cui

6.5.25 Mei Gui Sa Jin

6.5.26 Zi Guan Yin Xian

6.5.16 Zi Gong Chun Xiu

6.5.5 Hong Guan Xiang Cui

6.5.13 Hong Guan Yu Zhu

6.5.7 Cheng Xin

6.5.10 Yan Chun

6.5.12 Zi Guan Yu Zhu

6.5.15 Xiang Yan

6.5.8 Liu Chun

6.5.9 Hong Zhou Chou

6.6.8 Lan Tian Piao Yun

6.6#3

6.6.1 Hong Lou Fei Yan

6.5.17 Fu Li Hong

6.5.14 Zi Jin Cheng

6.5.3 Qing Si Wan Lu

6.5.6 Hong Lou Wan Zhang

6.6.2 Gong Deng

6.6.7 Lan Lou Yu Dai

6.6#4

6.6.4 Hong Zhuang Su Guo

6.5.25 Mei Gui Sa Jin

6.6.3 Li Xiang

6.6.5 Lian Chun

7.1#2

7.1#3

7.1.1 Ye Guang Bei

6.5.24 Wu Cai Zi Xiu Qiu

6.6#2

6.6.3 Li Xiang

6.6.6 Xiang Lu Zi Yan

7.1.2 Hei Xuan Feng

7.1.3 Mo Hai Yin Zhou

7.1.6 Bing Xin Ye Guang Bei

7.1.5 Hei Feng Die

7.1.4 Hei Yuan Shuai

7.1#1

7.1.5 Hei Feng Die

7.1.9 Zi Die Ying Feng

7.1.10 Zi Die Chu Yu

7.2#1

7.3.2 Hei Zhen Zhu

7.5.1 Mo Yun

7.4.3 Mo Guan Yin Xian

7.5.2 Mo Guan

7.1.7 Hei Zhou Chou

7.4.1 Hei Tian E

7.3.2 Hei Zhen Zhu

7.2.1 Da Ban Zi

7.2.2 Hei Wang Zi

7.3.1 Zi Ta Yan Yun

7.4#1

7.4.2 Mo Chou

7.1.8 Zao Yuan Hong

7.4.1 Hei Tian E

8.1.8 Lan Feng Zhan Chi

8.1.6 Hong Hai Dan Xin

8.1.3 Zi Ye Fen

8.1.13 Guan Huai

8.1#16

8.1#1

8.1#2

8.1#3

8.1#4

8.1#5

8.1#6

8.1#7

8.1#8

8.1#9

8.1#10

8.1#11

8.1#12

8.1#13

8.1#14

8.1#15

8.1.1 Tian Jing Nu Lang

8.1.2 Bing Xin Fen Lian

8.1.4 Fen Jin Yu Zhu

8.1.5 Zong Ban Fen

8.1.7 Tao Yuan

8.1.9 Lan Hai Ying Yue

8.1.10 Tao Yuan Yin Ge

8.1.11 Lan He Dian Yun

8.1.12 Lan Tian

8.2.1 Jin Ye Fen

8.2.2 Du Juan Ti Xue

8.5.1 Lan Shan Hu

8.3#1

8.3#2

8.3.2 Lan Hai

8.3#3

8.3.5 Wu Long Jiao Hai

8.3.4 Jin Yu Xi Shui

8.2.1 Jin Ye Fen

8.2.3 Fen Rong Cha Cui

8.3#4

8.3.1 Li Chun

8.3.3 Lan Fu Rong

8.4#1

8.4.1 Mo Shu Shi

8.4#2

8.4.4 Lan E Rong

8.4.3 Lan Zhen Zhu

8.4.2 San Hua Nu

8.5.2 Lan Guan Yu Zhu

8.5.3 Lan Ta Xiang Cui

9.1.13 Ri Yue Tong Hui

9.1#8

9.1#2

9.1.11 Hui Die

9.1.12 Hui He

9.1.7 Zhou Lang

9.1.5 Hei Hai Feng Yun

9.1.10 He Hua Deng

9.1#10

9.1.13 Ri Yue Tong Hui

9.1.14 Han Hai Bing Xin

9.1#1

9.1#3

9.1#4

9.1.9 He Tang Ying Yue

9.1.9 He Tang Ying Yue

9.1.9 He Tang Ying Yue

9.1#5

9.1#6

9.1#9

9.1#11

9.1#12

9.1#13

9.1#14

9.1#15

9.1#16

9.1#17

9.1#18

9.1#19

9.1.5 Hei Hai Feng Yun

9.1.9 He Tang Ying Yue

9.1.8 Hei Rui Die

9.1#20

9.1#21

9.1#22

9.1#23

9.1#24

9.1#25

9.1#26

9.1#27

9.1#28

9.1#29

9.1#30

9.1#31

9.1#32

9.1#33

9.1#34

9.1#35

9.1#36

9.1#37

9.1#38

9.1#39

9.1#40

9.1#41

9.1#42

9.1#43

9.1#44

9.1#45

9.1#46

9.1.1 Xue Hai Fei Hong

9.1.2 Fen He Dian Yun

9.1.3 Xin He Ying Ri

9.1.4 Long Yuan Xia Nu

9.1.6 Zong Ban Fen He

9.1.13 Ri Yue Tong Hui

9.2#2

9.2#3

9.2#1

9.2.4 Fo Guang Lan

9.2#10

9.2.1 Fen Bi Lan Xi

9.2.8 Da Mo Feng Yun

9.2.4 Fo Guang Lan

9.2.6 Wang Gong Yuan

9.2.3 Qiao Zhuang

9.2#4

9.2#5

9.2#6

9.2#7

9.2#8

9.2#9

9.2.2 Bo Si Nu

9.2.5 Bao Lian Deng

9.2.7 Qiang Wei Lan

9.3#4

9.3#2

9.3#3

9.3#1

9.3.1 Bo Si Shao Nu

9.4#1

9.3.3 Chang E Ben Yue

9.3.5 Chun You

9.3.4 Tai Kong Ren

9.4.6 He Ping Er Qiao

9.4.4 Fen Lou Dian Jin

9.4.6 He Ping Er Qiao

9.4.7 Feng Yan Si Qi

9.4.3 Fen Zhen Zhu

9.4.2 Qi Lian Zhao Hui

9.4#2

9.4#3

9.4.1 Fo Zhu

9.4.5 Yu Pan Fen Zhu

9.4.8 Bao Dao Shu Guang

9.4.9 Man Yuan Chun Se

9.5#3

9.5.2 Gu Sha Jin Zhong

9.5.8 Qi Lian Nong Xia

9.5.13 Jin Pao Yu Pei

9.5.9 Cai Yun Ge

9.5.14 Da Mo Tuo Ling

9.5.4 Cai Lou

9.5.7 Cai Guan Yin Dai

9.5.10 Ping Fen Qiu Se

9.5.10 Ping Fen Qiu Se

9.5.12 Shui Man Jin Shan

9.5.5 Lan Xia Fei Yun

9.5.11 Qi Lian Wan Xia

9.5.4 Cai Lou

9.5.1 Luan Yun Fei Du

9.5#2

9.6.5 He Ping Tian Shi

9.5.3 Long Yuan Zhuang Shi

9.5.6 Lan Yun Qian Li

9.6.5 He Ping Tian Shi

9.6#1

9.6.2 Lan Shan Chong Lou

9.6.3 Xiang Yi Si Hai

9.6#3

9.6#2

9.6.1 Fen Tai Xiang Cui

9.6.4 Er Qiao Li Xiang

SECTION 4

NOTES AND LISTS

---

11. MAIN CULTIVAR LIST AND NOTES

11.1 Main cultivar list in numerical order, with basic cultivar form details

Columns one to three give the reference number for each cultivar, its correct cultivar name and the basic meaning in English of the Chinese name. The fourth column gives the period during which the cultivar was named and introduced and the person who named the cultivar. The fifth column indicates growth characteristics of the cultivar where it has been observed to be significantly different from average.

In column three * indicates there is a note in 11.2.

In column four CDZ denotes Chen Dezhong,
              CFH denotes Chen Fuhui,
              CFF denotes Chen Fufei,
              HT   denotes Hong Tao.

              1 denotes before 1985,
              2 denotes 1986 to 1992,
              3 denotes 1993 to 1994,
              4 denotes 1995 to 2002,
              5 denotes 2003 to 2005.

In column five E and L denote Early and Late flowering,
              V denotes Vigorous,
              S and U denote Spreading and Upright growth habit

Paeonia Gansu Group   'Fen Mo Deng Chang'

粉墨登场

number	*pinyin* name	basic meaning	date	form		
1.1.1	Bing Shan Xue Lian	Icy Mountain Snow Lotus	2CDZ	E		
1.1.2	Shu Sheng Peng Mo	Scholar Holding Ink*	2CDZ		V	
1.1.3	Bai Bi Lan Xia	White and Blue Clouds	2CDZ		V	S
1.1.4	Hei Fa Nu Lang	Black-haired Girl	2CDZ			
1.1.5	Xue Hai Bing Xin	Snow Sea Icy Heart*	2CDZ			
1.1.6	Da Xue Hai Bing Xin	Big Snow Sea Icy Heart	5CFH			
1.1.7	Yu Feng Dian Tou	Jade Phoenix Nodding Head	2CDZ			
1.1.8	Bai He Liang Chi	White Crane Showing Wings	2CDZ			U
1.1.9	Wu Fa Lan Dai	Black Hair Blue Belt	2CDZ			
1.1.10	Xue Hai Chen Guang	Snow Sea Morning Light	3CDZ			
1.1.11	Yin Pan Zi Zhu	Silver Plate Purple Pearl	3CDZ			
1.1.12	Ju He San Bian	Giant Lotus Three Changes	3CDZ			
1.1.13	Mu Chun Bai	Late Spring White	5CFH	L		
1.1.14	Hei Long Tan	Black Dragon's Pond	3CDZ			
1.1.15	Yi Dian Mo	Spot of Ink	3CDZ		V	U
1.1.16	Yi Ding Mo	Ink Stick*	3CDZ		V	
1.1.17	Yu Long Bei	Jade Dragon's Cup	3CDZ		V	
1.1.18	Wu Kong Xiu Xing	Wu Kong's Meditation*	3CDZ			
1.1.19	Xiong Mao	Panda*	3CDZ			
1.1.20	Hei Bai Fen Ming	Black and White Clear Division	3CDZ	L	V	
1.1.21	Zhong Xing Peng Yue	Many Stars Holding the Moon	2CDZ			
1.1.22	Bei Ji Xiong	Polar Bear	3CDZ		V	S
1.1.23	Xue Hai Fang Xin	Snow Sea Sweet Heart	2CDZ			
1.1.24	Xue Hai Dan Xin	Snow Sea Red Heart	4CDZ			
1.1.25	Xiao Bai Yu	Small White Jade	2CDZ			
1.1.26	Yan Huang Er Nu	Children of the Yellow River*	5CFH			
1.1.27	Hei Fa Dan Xin	Black Hair Red Heart	2CDZ			
1.1.28	Wu Jiao Xing	Five-pointed Star*	2CFF			
1.1.29	Yan Hua Chu Fang	Firework Display Begins	2CDZ			
1.1.30	Yin Die Fei Wu	Silver Butterfly Flying	2CDZ			
1.1.31	Pan Pan	Pan Pan*	2CDZ			
1.1.32	Mo Ban Yin Guang	Magic Blotch Silver Light	2CDZ			
1.1.33	Fu Ai	Father's Love	2CFH			
1.1.34	Ai	Love	5CFH			
1.1.35	Yin Pan Tuo Gui	Anemone on Silver Plate	2CDZ			
1.1.36	Mei Ran Gong	Handsome Bearded Man*	5CFH			
1.1.37	Tong Xin Tong De	One Heart One Mind*	3CDZ			
1.1.38	Cao Chuan Jie Jian	Straw Boats Borrow Arrows*	3CDZ			
1.1.39	Bei Ji Guang	Aurora Borealis	3CDZ			
1.1.40	Xin Xing	New Star	2CDZ			
1.1.41	Hong Xia Ying Xue	Red Cloud Reflected in Snow	2CDZ			
1.1.42	Tu Xing	Earth Star*	5CFH			
1.1.43	Fo Guang Fen	Buddhist-light Pink	4CDZ			
1.1.44	Zhao Jun Fei Yun	Zhao Jun's Blushes*	4CDZ			
1.1.45	Bei Dou Xing	The Plough*	5CFH		V	
1.1.46	Da Mo Gu Yan	Great Desert Solitary Smoke	3CDZ			
1.1.47	Ao Yun Zhi Guang	Olympic Games Flame	5CFH			
1.1.48	Fen Die Chu Yu	Pink Butterfly Young Wings	2CDZ			
1.1.49	Yu Shan Guan Jin	Feather Fan Silk Braid*	5CFH			

1.1.50	Xue Yu Zhi Huan	The Joys of Snow	2CDZ			
1.1.51	Hong Zong Lie Ma	Red-maned Horse	5CFH			
1.1.52	Ju Ban Fen	Huge Blotch Pink	5CFH			S
1.1.53	Jin Si Bai	Gold Thread White	5CFH			
1.1.54	Jin Ye Bai	Gold-leaved White	5CFH	L		
1.1.55	Dian Jin Yan Wei Fen	Gold-dotted Swallow-tail Pink	5CFH			
1.1.56	Zong Ban Bai	Brown-blotched White	5CFH			
1.1.57	Guan Ai	Loving Care	5CFH	L		
1.1.58	Xue Hua	Snowflake	5CFH			
1.2.1	Yao Tai Jiu Nu	Nine Girls at Yao Tai*	3CDZ			
1.2.2	Yin Yang Shan	Yin and Yang Fan*	3CDZ			
1.2.3	Hong Chi Wei Bo	Red Pond Small Wave	3CDZ			
1.2.4	Ji Gong	Ji Gong*	5CFH	L		
1.2.5	Yu Tang Chun	Jade Hall Spring*	3CDZ			
1.2.6	Re Xue Qing Chun	Hot-blooded Youth	3CDZ			
1.2.7	Hong Fa Mo Nu	Red-haired Magic Lady	2CDZ			
1.2.8	Yin Hai Hong Bo	Silver Sea Red Wave	3CDZ			
1.2.9	Xiu Fa Pi Jian	Beautiful Hair Covering Shoulders	4CDZ	L	V	
1.2.10	Qin Jin Zhi Hao	Qin and Jin United*	2CDZ		V	
1.2.11	Fen Lou Cha Cui	Pink Pavilion with Emeralds	2CDZ			
1.2.12	Qing Hai Hu Yin Bo	Silver Swell on Qing Hai Lake*	2CDZ		V	
1.2.13	Yuan Yang Pu	Mandarin Duck Music*	2CDZ	L	V	
1.2.14	Yu Lu Lian Dan	Jade Stove Makes Pills of Immortality*	2CDZ	L	V	
1.2.15	Long Gong De Bao	Dragon Palace Treasure*	5CFH	L	V	S
1.2.16	Hong Guang Man Mian	Ruddy Complexion*	5CFH	L		
1.3.1	Gui Fu Ren	Chic Lady	2CDZ			
1.3.2	Fei Tian	Flying in the Sky	2CDZ			U
1.3.3	Fen Mian Tao Sai	Pink Face Peach Cheek	3CDZ			
1.3.4	Xiao Xue	Little Snow*	2CDZ			
1.3.5	Xue Li Cang Jin	Gold Hidden in Snow	2CDZ		V	U
1.3.6	He Luo Yin Hai	Crane Landing on Silver Sea	2CDZ			
1.3.7	Lian Hua Shan	Lotus Mountain*	2CDZ			
1.3.8	Yu Nu Tan Hai	Jade Girl Exploring the Sea	3CDZ	L	V	
1.3.9	Yin Lou Hui Cai	Silver Pagoda Colourful Pictures	3CDZ			
1.3.10	Bei Ji Hu	Arctic Fox	3CDZ			
1.3.11	Xue Shan Yu Hui	Snow Mountain Evening Glow	2CDZ			
1.3.12	Xue Zhan Chang Ban Po	Battle at Chang Ban Pass*	2CDZ			
1.3.13	Xue Shan Fei Hong	Rainbow over Snow Mountain	5CFH			
1.3.14	Ba Jiao Shan	Palm-leaf Fan*	3CDZ			
1.3.15	Hong Ban Ju Hua Bai	Red Blotch Chrysanthemum White	5CFH			
1.3.16	Bing Shan Dian Yun	Icy Mountain Rosy Mist	5CFH			U
1.3.17	Bai Yi Da Xia	White-coated Cavalier*	5CFH	L	V	U
1.3.18	Fen Yu	Pink Jade	1CDZ			
1.3.19	Li Hua Zui Jiu	Tipsy Li Hua*	2CDZ		V	U
1.3.20	Yu Guan Cai Dai	Jade Crown Colourful Belt	5CFH			
1.4.1	Qi E Wo Bing	Penguins on the Ice	3CDZ			
1.4.2	Xue Shan Jin Ding	Snow Mountain Gold Summit	1CDZ		V	
1.4.3	Xing Long Rui Xue	Good Snow on Xing Long Mountain*	2CDZ		V	
1.4.4	Zhen Zhu Bai	Pearl White	2CDZ			
1.4.5	Jiao Yu	Graceful Girl	2CDZ			
1.4.6	Dian Jin Bai Yan Wei	White Swallow Tail Speckled Gold	3CDZ			S

1.4.7	Yan Wei Bai	Swallow Tail White	3CDZ		V	
1.4.8	Jin Bo Dang Yang	Gentle Gold Waves	1CDZ			
1.4.9	Ju Hua Huang	Chrysanthemum Yellow	2CDZ			
1.4.10	Qi Lian Cai Hong	Qi Lian Mountain Rainbow	2CDZ			
1.4.11	Fen Guan Jin Zhu	Pink Crown Gold Pearl	2CDZ	E	V	
1.4.12	Ju Hua Fen	Chrysanthemum Pink	1CDZ			
1.4.13	Liu Yao Bai	Slender White	5CFH			
1.4.14	Yu Lou Pi Cai	Coloured Jade Palace	2CDZ	L		
1.4.15	Yin Shan Dan Xia	Silver Mountain Red Clouds	3CDZ			
1.5.1	Yu Ban Xiu Qiu	Jade Petal Embroidered Glow	2CDZ	E	V	
1.5.2	Fen Bi Sheng Hui	Glorious Pink and Green	3CDZ	L	V	
1.5.3	Bai Zhang Bing	Great Ice Cliff	2CDZ		V	
1.5.4	Jiang Tai Gong Diao Yu	Wise Jiang Fishes*	5CFH	L	V	
1.5.5	Jin Cheng Ming Yue	Gold City Clear Moon*	2CDZ		V	
1.5.6	Yu Guan Jin Zhu	Jade Crown Gold Pearl	2CDZ			
1.5.7	Xing Yun	Star Cloud	2CDZ			
1.5.8	Tian Shan Ri Chu	Sunrise at Tian Mountain	2CDZ	L	V	U
1.5.9	Xing Guang Can Lan	Star Light Splendour	2CDZ			
1.5.10	Yu Lou Shan Jin	Jade Building Shining Gold	3CDZ			
1.5.11	Feng Chu	Young Phoenix	3CDZ	L		U
1.5.12	Jiao Mei	Favourite Beauty	5CDZ			
1.5.13	Yu Guan Hei Fa	Jade Crown Black Hair	3CDZ			
1.5.14	Yu Guan Lan Dai	Jade Crown Blue Belt	3CDZ	L	V	S
1.5.15	Xue Shan Wan Xia	Snow Mountain Sunset Glow	3CDZ		V	
1.5.16	Huo Fo Ju Shou	Gathering of Living Buddhas	3CDZ			
1.5.17	Yin Ju Cui Rui	Silver Chrysanthemum Green Stamens	3CDZ			
1.5.18	Huang He Lou	Yellow River Pagoda	3CDZ	E		
1.5.19	Yin Zhuang Su Guo	Range of Snowy Mountains	5CFH		V	
1.5.20	Long Yuan Xue	Snow on Gansu Plateau	5CFH			U
1.5.21	Yu Guan Xiang Cui	Jade Crown Inlaid with Emeralds	3CDZ			
1.5.22	Xue Yuan Zao Chun	Snowy Plain in Early Spring	3CDZ		V	
1.5.23	Yu Lou Xiang Cui	Jade Pavilion Inlaid with Emeralds	3CDZ			
1.5.24	Bai Yi Nu Xia	White-coated Martial Arts Girl	4CDZ			
1.5.25	Fen Ge Miao Jin	Pink Pavilion Gold Paint	2CDZ			
1.5.26	Xiao Lou Dian Yun	Small Pavilion Speckled Colour	3CDZ			
1.5.27	Lan Hua Nu	Orchid Girl	5CFH			
1.6.1	Xue Ye Han Yan	Snow Wilderness Cold Smoke	1CDZ			
1.6.2	Yu Lou Cang Jiao	Jade Building Hidden Maidens	2CDZ			
1.6.3	Bei Guo Feng Guang	Northern Landscapes*	1CDZ		V	
1.6.4	Xue Yuan Xing Huo	Snow Plateau Twinkling Lights	5CFH			
1.6.5	Yue Zhao Kun Lun	Moonlight on Kun Lun Mountain	2CDZ		V	
1.6.6	Bai Pao Jin Dai	White Robe Silk Belt	3CDZ	L	V	U
1.6.7	Wu Duo Jin Hua	Five Gold Maidens*	3CDZ			
1.6.8	Kun Lun Qiu Se	Autumn Colour in Kun Lun Mountains	2CDZ			
1.6.9	Yin Bai He	Silver Lily	2CDZ		V	
1.6.10	Bai Yun Hong Xia	White Clouds and Red Clouds	3CDZ		V	S
1.6.11	Tian Gao Yun Dan	High Sky Faint Cloud	3CDZ			
1.6.12	Gao Lou Cang Jiao	High Building Hidden Maidens	5CFH	L	V	U
1.6.13	Sai Bai He	Better than Bai He*	5CFH			
1.6.14	Bai Xiu Qiu	Peace White Embroidered Globe	3CDZ			
1.6.15	Yan Rao Bai Ta	Smoke Encircling White Pagoda*	3CDZ			

2.1.1	Huang Lian	Yellow Lotus	5CFH			
2.1.2	Yin Si Bai	Silver Thread White	5CFH			
2.1.3	Yu He Dian Yun	Blushing Jade Lotus	3CDZ			
2.1.4	Pan Deng	Aiming High	5CFH			
2.1.5	Xiao Xue Hai Bing Xin	Small Snow Sea Icy Heart	5CFH			
2.1.6	Xue Hai Yin Zhen	Snow Sea Silver Needle	3CDZ	L		
2.1.7	Hong Shu Lin	Red Forest	5CFH			
2.1.8	Huang He	The Yellow River	2CDZ			
2.1.9	Huang Tu Gao Yuan	Yellow Earth High Plateau	2CDZ		V	
2.1.10	Huang Shan Chen Xi	Yellow Mountain Morning Glory*	2CDZ			
2.3.1	Yu Guan Yue	Moon Above Jade Pass	2CDZ			
2.3.2	Gao Yuan Shen Qiu	High Plateau Late Autumn	5CFH			
2.3.3	Wan Xue Ying Chun	Late Snow Welcomes Spring	2CDZ			S
2.4.1	Juan Bian Huang	Curled Edge Yellow	5CFH			
2.5.1	Ju Hua Bai	Chrysanthemum White	1CDZ	E	V	
2.5.2	Huang Yun	Yellow Clouds	5CFH		V	S
2.5.3	Bing Shan Cang Yu	Icy Mountain Hides Jade	2CDZ	E	V	
2.6.1	Huang Jin Yu Zhui	Yellow Scarf Jade Tassel	5CFH			
3.1.1	Chun Dao Long Yuan	Spring Arriving at Gansu Plateau	4CDZ	L		
3.5.1	Li Ren Zhuang	Beauty's Make-up	5CFH			
3.5.2	Jing Yu Dian Cui	Crystal Jade Speckled Emerald	2CDZ	L		
3.5.3	Fen Yu Dian Cui	Pink Jade Speckled Emerald	4CDZ			
3.5.4	Bing Shan Fei Cui	Icy Mountain Green Jade	5CFH			U
4.1.1	Fen He	Pink Lotus	1CDZ	E	V	
4.1.2	Fen Chi Ying Yue	Pink Pond Reflecting the Moon	3CDZ		V	S
4.1.3	Hong Hai Yin Zhou	Red Sea Silver Boat	2CDZ			
4.1.4	Mo Chi Ying Yue	Black Pond Reflecting the Moon	3CDZ			
4.1.5	Hong Lian	Red Lotus	1CDZ			
4.1.6	Xing Gao Cai Lie	Exhilaration*	5CFH			
4.1.7	Lue Shi Fen Dai	A Little Make-up	3CDZ		V	
4.1.8	Ying Ri He Hua	Lotus Flower Reflecting the Sun	2CDZ	L		
4.1.9	Fo Guang Hong	Buddhist-light Red	4CDZ			
4.1.10	Mo Chi Yan Xia	Black Pond Smoky Cloud	5CFH			
4.1.11	Long Yuan Fen	Gansu Plateau Pink	5CFH			
4.1.12	Tie Mian Wu Si	Incorruptible Judge*	2CDZ		V	
4.1.13	Jiao Yang	Blazing Sun	2CDZ			
4.1.14	Gui Zhong Shao Fu	Young Wife at Home	5CFH			
4.2.1	Mo Nu	Sourceress	5CFH			
4.2.2	Xue Yuan Yu Hui	Snowy Plain Sunset	2CDZ			
4.2.3	Jiu Zhou Tai	Nine Continent Platform*	4CDZ			
4.2.4	Hong Hai Yin Lang	Red Ocean Silver Waves	4CDZ			
4.2.5	Ne Zha Nao Hai	Ne Zha Overturns the Sea*	5CFH			
4.2.6	Er Long Xi Zhu	Two Dragons Play with a Pearl*	2CDZ			
4.2.7	Wan Hua Hong	Late Flower Red	4CDZ			
4.2.8	Wan Hua Zi	Late Flower Purple	5CFH	L	V	
4.3.1	Fo Guang	Buddhist Light	2CDZ			
4.3.2	Fen Mo Deng Chang	Pink Ink on to the Stage*	3CDZ			
4.3.3	Tan Hua Fen	Ephemeral Pink	2CDZ		V	S
4.3.4	Wen Jun Xin Meng	Wen Jun's New Dream*	3CDZ			
4.3.5	Long Yuan Er Qiao	Gansu Plateau Two Beauties	5CFH			
4.3.6	Da Qian Shi Jie	The Boundless Universe	5CFH			

4.3.7	He Tang Qiu Bo	Lotus Pond Autumn Wave	3CDZ		
4.3.8	Jin Cheng Wan Xia	Gold City Evening Clouds*	2CDZ		
4.3.9	He Ping Fen	Peace Pink	5CFH	V	
4.3.10	Qiang Wei Fen	Rose Pink	5CFH		
4.4.1	Yu Lou Fen	Jade Pavilion Pink	3CDZ		
4.4.2	Qian Zi Bai Tai	Thousand Posture Hundred Forms*	2CDZ		
4.4.3	Fen Guan Cai Die	Pink Crown Colourful Butterfly	2CDZ		
4.4.4	Fen Guan Yu Dai	Pink Crown Jade Belt	2CDZ		
4.4.5	Fen Yu San Tai	Pink Jade Three Tiers	2CDZ		S
4.4.6	Zi Xia Dong Zhao	Purple Glow Eastern Light	3CDZ		
4.4.7	Xue Shan Chui Yan	Snow Mountain Cooking Smoke	2CDZ		
4.4.8	Hong Yi Nu Lang	Lady in Red	2CDZ		S
4.4.9	Qing Chun	Youth	1CDZ		
4.4.10	Dai Yu Zang Hua	Dai Yu Buries Flowers*	3CDZ		S
4.4.11	Zhen Zhu Nu	Pearl Girl	2CDZ		
4.4.12	Zi Yun Feng	Purple Cloud Summit	5CFH		
4.5.1	Fen Yan Jiao	Pink Graceful Lady	2CDZ	L	
4.5.2	Xia Guang Wan Li	Morning Light from Afar*	5CFH		
4.5.3	Xia Ran Qing Shan	Morning Glow on Green Mountain	5CFH		
4.5.4	Mu Yang Nu	Shepherdess	5CFH		
4.5.5	Shen Nu	Goddess	5CFH		
4.5.6	Zi Xian Nu	Purple Thread Lady	5CFH		
4.5.7	Chang E Shu Xiu	Chang E Unrolls Sleeves*	2CDZ	V	
4.5.8	Xiao Xia	Martial Arts Youngster	5CFH		
4.5.9	Zui Fei	Tipsy Concubine*	4CFH		
4.5.10	Jiao Rong Chu Lu	Beautiful Complexion Emerging	5CFH		
4.5.11	Zhong Jie Mei	Many Sisters	3CDZ		
4.5.12	Fen Lou Dan Xin	Pink Pavilion Red Heart	5CFH		U
4.5.13	Tao Hua Yuan	Peach Blossom Source	3CDZ		
4.5.14	Jin Huan Fen	Gold Circle Pink	5CDZ		
4.5.15	Ju Yuan Xin Xiu	Orange Garden New Talent	5CFH		
4.5.16	Hong Yun Shan	Red Cloud Mountain	3CDZ		
4.5.17	Hong Xian Nu	Red Thread Woman	2CDZ	V	
4.5.18	Fen Yan Wei	Pink Swallow Tail	3CDZ	L	
4.5.19	Qing Feng Wan Xia	Green Summit Night Light	5CFH		
4.5.20	Lan Xian Diao Jin Chan	Gold Toad Hanging on a Blue Thread*	3CDZ	V	
4.5.21	Fei Xiang Yu Zhou	Fly Towards the Universe*	4CDZ		U
4.5.22	Tian Mi De Meng	Sweet Dreams	1CDZ	V	
4.5.23	Li Fu Ren	Mrs Li*	2CDZ	V	
4.5.24	Tao Yuan Ju Hui	Peach Garden Meeting*	2CDZ		
4.5.25	Hong Lou Dian Jin	Red Pavilion Speckled Gold	2CDZ E	V	U
4.5.26	Feng Guan Yu Zhu	Phoenix Crown Jade Pearl	5CFH L	V	
4.5.27	He Ping Hong	Peace Red	3CFY		
4.5.28	Lan Guan Yu Dai	Blue Crown Jade Belt	5CFH	V	
4.6.1	Chu E Zhan Chi	Young Goose Spreading Wings	3CDZ		
4.6.2	Lan Xian Nu	Blue Thread Woman	2CDZ	V	
4.6.3	Li Xia Fen	Li Xia Pink*	2CDZ	L	
4.6.4	Fen Guan Cai Dai	Pink Crown Colourful Belt	2CDZ	V	S
4.6.5	Shen Guang Yu Lu	Morning Dew	5CFH		
4.6.6	Feng Juan Can Yun	Wind Gathering Scattered Clouds	5CFH		
4.6.7	Chun Jiang Yan Bo	Smoke-like Wave on Chun River	2CDZ		

4.6.8	Feng Zi Xiu Se	Graceful Bearing Charming Colour	2CDZ	L		
4.6.9	Lan Yue	Blue Moon	5CFH			
4.6.10	Yu Zhong Fen	Yu Zhong Pink*	3CDZ			
4.6.11	Hong Lou Yu Ding	Red Pavilion Jade Roof	5CFH	E		
4.6.12	Tian Shan Xia Nu	Martial Arts Girls on Tian Mountain	5CFH			
4.6.13	Fen Ge Piao Cai	Pink Pavilion Bright Colours	3CDZ		V	U
4.6.14	Tao Hua Nu	Peach Blossom Girl	2CDZ		V	
4.6.15	Zhong Shan Feng Yu	Wind and Rain on Zhong Mountain	2CDZ			
4.6.16	Tao Hong Xiu Qiu	Peach Red Colourful Globe	2CDZ		V	
4.6.17	Jin Cheng Lan	Gold City Blue	2CDZ			
4.6.18	He Ping Lan	Peace Blue	1CDZ			
4.6.19	Mai Ji Shan Yan Yun	Mai Ji Mountain Smokey Cloud*	2CDZ			
4.6.20	Yin Xian Diao Jin Gui	Fishing for Gold Turtle with a Silver Thread*	3CDZ			
4.6.21	Diao Chan Bai Yue	Diao Chan Bows to the Moon*	1CDZ		V	
4.6.22	He Ping Hong Xiu Qiu	Peace Red Embroidered Globe	3CDZ			
4.6.23	Fen Yu Sheng Hui	Glorious Jade Pink	5CFH			
4.6.24	Fei Yan Gui Chao	Swallow Returns to the Nest	3CDZ			
4.6.25	Zi Guan Yu Dai	Purple Crown Jade Belt	5CFH			
5.1.1	Long Yuan Hong	Gansu Plateau Red	2CDZ			
5.1.2	Hong Hai Jin Dao	Red Ocean Gold Island	4CDZ			
5.1.3	Ju Yuan Shao Nu	Orange Garden Young Girl	3CDZ			
5.1.4	Xi Yang Hong	Setting Sun Red	3CDZ			
5.1.5	Re Lie	Warmth	2CDZ			
5.1.6	Xi Qing You Yu	Happy Celebrations Continue	2CDZ			
5.1.7	Hong Qi Man Juan	Red Flags Spreading in Triumph	4CDZ			
5.1.8	Shen Guang	Divine Light	5CFH	L		
5.1.9	Zi Jin Huan	Purple Gold Circle	4CDZ			
5.1.10	Xi Yu Bing Chuan	Glacier in the West	5CFH	E	V	
5.2.1	Zi Kui Xiang Ri	Purple Sunflower Facing the Sun	4CDZ			
5.2.2	Bing Xin Zi	Icy Heart Purple	2CDZ			S
5.2.3	Yan Li	Dazzling Beauty	2CDZ			
5.2.4	Hong Guang Ying Tian	Red Sky Light	5CFH			
5.2.5	Mo Hai Yin Bo	Black Sea Silver Wave	3CDZ			
5.3.1	Zi Ling Long	Exquisite Purple	2CDZ	E	V	
5.3.2	Zi Yuan Yang	Purple Mandarin Duck	2CDZ			
5.3.3	Zi Hai Yin Bo	Purple Sea Silver Wave	2CDZ			
5.3.4	Mo Guan Yu Zhu	Black Crown Jade Pearl	5CFH			
5.4.1	Feng Xian	Dedication	2CDZ	E		
5.4.2	Zi Ta Dian Jin	Purple Tower Speckled Gold	3CDZ		V	
5.5.1	Hong Lou Jin Chai	Red Pavilion Gold Hairpin	5CFH			
5.5.2	Chen Hong Yi Hao	Chen Hong Number One*	5CFH			
5.5.3	Li Shi Mo Kui	Best Black Li*	2CDZ	E		
5.5.4	Zi Zhou Chou	Purple Silk	2CDZ			
5.5.5	Xuan Nu Gong	Xuan Nu's Palace*	5CFH			
5.6.1	Hong Tai Yin Ge	Red Tower Silver Balcony	4CDZ		V	U
6.1.1	Shui Xing	Water Star*	4CDZ			
6.1.2	You Yi	Friendship	3CDZ			
6.1.3	Hong Qian Niu	Girl Leading a Cow	5CFH			
6.1.4	Guang Hui Li Cheng	Glorious Journey	2CDZ			
6.1.5	Jin Cheng Nu Lang	Gold City Lady	2CDZ			
6.1.6	Zi Hai Yin Guang	Purple Sea Silver Light	4CDZ			

6.1.7	Bao Gong	Judge Bao Gong*	5CFH		
6.1.8	Lan He	Blue Lotus	1CDZ		
6.1.9	Nan Hai Jin Dao	South Sea Gold Island	3CDZ		
6.1.10	Bing Xin Lan He	Icy Heart Blue Lotus	4CDZ		
6.1.11	Juan Bian Lan He	Curled Edge Blue Lotus	3CDZ		U
6.1.12	Lan Mo Shuang Hui	Blue Black Double Glory	1CDZ		
6.2.1	Mu Ai	Mother's Love	3CDZ		
6.2.2	Gao Gan Hong	Splendid Red Sorghum	4CDZ		
6.2.3	Hong Hai Yin Bo	Red Ocean Silver Wave	2CDZ	E	
6.2.4	Zi Yan	Purple Ink Stone	2CDZ	E	
6.2.5	Gu Cheng Xiang Hui	Meeting in Ancient City*	2CDZ	E	
6.3.1	Huai Nian	Cherished Memories	1CDZ		
6.3.2	Hong Hai Feng Yun	Red Ocean Storm Clouds	3CDZ		
6.3.3	Hong Hai Yang	Red Ocean	3CDZ		
6.3.4	Tao Hua Shan	Peach Flower Fan*	2CDZ		
6.3.5	Chun Man Ren Jian	Spring Throughout the World	3CDZ		
6.3.6	Hong Zhen Zhu	Red Pearls	3CDZ		
6.3.7	Hong Yu Fan Lang	Red Rain Giant Waves	3CDZ		
6.3.8	Tao Rong	Peach Complexion	1CDZ		
6.3.9	Jin Cheng Hong	Gold City Red	5CFH	V	U
6.3.10	Hong Yi Shao Nu	Girl in Red	5CFH		
6.3.11	Xiu Lou Xiang Cui	Graceful Pavilion Emerald Inlay	2CDZ		
6.3.12	Lan Zhang Cai Wei	Blue Net Coloured Curtain	3CDZ	E	V
6.3.13	Xiao Ban Lan Xiu Qiu	Small Blotch Blue Embroidered Globe	3CD		
6.3.14	Zhou Mei Gui	Silk Rose	3CD		
6.3.15	Chen Yuan Zi	Chen's Garden Purple	5CFH	L	V
6.3.16	Ri Mu Gui Tuo	Returning Camels at Sunset	2CDZ		
6.3.17	Yi Jie Jin Lan	Pledge Friendship with Jin Lan	3CDZ		
6.3.18	Bao Shi Lan	Diamond Blue	1CDZ		S
6.4.1	Jing Shen Huan Fa	High Spirits*	2CDZ		
6.4.2	Hong Lou Cang Jin	Red Pavilion Hides Gold	2CDZ		
6.4.3	Hong Guan Yin Xian	Red Crown Silver Thread	2CDZ	V	
6.4.4	Hong Hai Qing Long	Red Ocean Green Dragon	2CDZ		
6.4.5	Jin Yu Man Shan	Gold Jade Mountain	3CDZ		
6.4.6	Chuan Jin Dai Yin	Wearing Gold and Silver	3CDZ		
6.4.7	Hong Yun Tu Qi	Sudden Red Cloud	3CDZ		
6.4.8	Lan Yu San Cai	Blue Jade Three Colours	2CDZ	V	U
6.4.9	Hong Xia Man Tian	Red Clouds Across the Sky	2CDZ	V	
6.4.10	Xiao Hong Ta	Small Red Tower	4CDZ		
6.4.11	Nong Xia Man Tian	Heavy Clouds Across the Sky	5CFH		
6.4.12	Zi Pao Chen Shuang	Purple Robe Morning Frost	3CDZ		
6.4.13	Zi Guan Yu Chi	Purple Crown Jade Wing	2CDZ	E	
6.4.14	Ju Hua Zi	Chrysanthemum Purple	3CD		
6.4.15	Zi Gui Yin Mai	Purple Osmanthus Silver Veins	3CDZ		U
6.4.16	Zi Zhu Lin	Purple Bamboo Forest	3CDZ	E	U
6.4.17	Hong Lou Jing Meng	Red Chambers Surprising Dream*	1CDZ		
6.4.18	Zi Jin Guan	Purple Gold Crown	2CDZ		
6.4.19	Jin Huan Yin Xian	Gold Circle Silver Thread	2CDZ		
6.4.20	Zi Ta Xiang Cui	Purple Tower Emerald Inlay	3CDZ		
6.4.21	Zi Zhen Zhu	Purple Pearl	5CFH		
6.4.22	Ju Hua Lan	Chrysanthemum Blue	2CDZ		

6.4.23	Geng Shang Yi Ceng Lou	Aim Higher Still*	3CDZ			
6.4.24	Lan Hai Yin Lang	Blue Sea Silver Wave	4CDZ			
6.4.25	Lan Tian Meng	Blue Sky Dream	1CDZ		V	
6.4.26	Wu Yan Liu Se	Multicoloured*	2CDZ		V	
6.4.27	Lan Hai Yin Bo	Blue Sea Silver Swell	2CDZ			
6.5.1	Tao Yuan Chun Se	Peach Garden Spring Colour	2CDZ			
6.5.2	Man Tang Hong	Complete Triumph*	3CDZ			
6.5.3	Qing Si Wan Lu	Luxuriant Black Hair	2CDZ		V	
6.5.4	Feng Cai	Glory	2CDZ			`
6.5.5	Hong Guan Xiang Cui	Red Crown Emerald Inlay	3CDZ			
6.5.6	Hong Lou Wan Zhang	Red Pavilion Great Height	3CDZ			
6.5.7	Cheng Xin	Devotion	2CDZ		V	
6.5.8	Li Chun	Prolong Spring	1CDZ	E		
6.5.9	Hong Zhou Chou	Red Silk	3CDZ			
6.5.10	Yan Chun	Gorgeous Spring	2CDZ	E	V	
6.5.11	Jiao Mei	Favourite Girl	3CDZ	E	V	
6.5.12	Zi Guan Yu Zhu	Purple Crown Jade Pearl	1CDZ			
6.5.13	Hong Guan Yu Zhu	Red Crown Jade Pearl	1CDZ			
6.5.14	Zi Jin Cheng	Purple Gold City	2CDZ			U
6.5.15	Xiang Yan	Fragrant and Beautiful	2CDZ			
6.5.16	Zi Gong Chun Xiu	Purple Palace Spring Beauty	1CDZ		V	
6.5.17	Fu Li Hong	Beautiful Rich Red*	2CDZ		V	
6.5.18	Zi Jin Ting	Pagoda on Zi Jin Mountain	3CDZ			
6.5.19	Zi Lou Cang Yu	Purple Pavilion Hides Jade	3CDZ			
6.5.20	Zi Lou Xiang Jin	Purple Pavilion Gold Inlay	3CDZ			
6.5.21	Zi Pao Yin Bian	Purple Robe Silver Edge	3CDZ			
6.5.22	Zi Luo Yin Wei	Purple and Silver Net	3CDZ			
6.5.23	Lan Xing Shan Cui	Blue Star Glittering Emerald	3CDZ			
6.5.24	Wu Cai Zi Xiu Qiu	Five Colour Purple Embroidered Globe	3CDZ			
6.5.25	Mei Gui Sa Jin	Scattered Rose Petals	1CDZ			
6.5.26	Zi Guan Yin Xian	Purple Crown Silver Thread	2CDZ	E		
6.6.1	Hong Lou Fei Yan	Red Pavilion Flying Swallow*	2CDZ			
6.6.2	Gong Deng	Palace Lantern	4CDZ			
6.6.3	Li Xiang	Idealism	2CDZ	E	V	
6.6.4	Hong Zhuang Su Guo	Plain Red Outfit	1CDZ			
6.6.5	Lian Chun	Missing the Spring	2CDZ	L	V	
6.6.6	Xiang Lu Zi Yan	Lu Mountain Purple Smoke*	1CDZ		V	S
6.6.7	Lan Lou Yu Dai	Blue Robe Jade Belt	2CDZ			
6.6.8	Lan Tian Piao Yun	Blue Sky Drifting Clouds	3CDZ			
7.1.1	Ye Guang Bei	Luminous Cup	1CDZ			
7.1.2	Hei Xuan Feng	Black Whirlwind	2CDZ	E	V	U
7.1.3	Mo Hai Yin Zhou	Black Sea Silver Boat	2CDZ			
7.1.4	Hei Yuan Shuai	Black Marshall	3CDZ	E		
7.1.5	Hei Feng Die	Black Phoenix Butterfly	3CD	E		U
7.1.6	Bing Xin Ye Guang Bei	Icy Heart Luminous Cup	4CDZ			
7.1.7	Hei Zhou Chou	Black Crepe Silk	5CFH			
7.1.8	Zao Yuan Hong	Date Garden Red	2CDZ			
7.1.9	Zi Die Ying Feng	Purple Butterfly Facing the Wind	2CDZ	E	V	
7.1.10	Zi Die Chu Yu	Purple Butterfly New Wings	3CDZ	E	V	
7.2.1	Da Ban Zi	Large Blotch Purple	4CDZ			
7.2.2	Hei Wang Zi	Black Prince	5CFH			

7.3.1	Zi Ta Yan Yun	Purple Tower Smoke Cloud	2CDZ			
7.3.2	Hei Zhen Zhu	Black Pearl	3CDZ	E		
7.4.1	Hei Tian E	Black Swan	2HT	E		
7.4.2	Mo Chou	Black Silk	3CDZ			
7.4.3	Mo Guan Yin Xian	Black Crown Silver Thread	2CDZ			
7.5.1	Mo Yun	Black Cloud	2CDZ	E		
7.5.2	Mo Guan	Black Crown	5CFH			
8.1.1	Tian Jing Nu Lang	Track and Field Sports Women	3CDZ			
8.1.2	Bing Xin Fen Lian	Icy Heart Pink Lotus	3CDZ			
8.1.3	Zi Ye Fen	Purple Leaf Pink	3CDZ			
8.1.4	Fen Jin Yu Zhu	Pink Scarf Jade Pearl	2CDZ			
8.1.5	Zong Ban Fen	Brown Blotch Pink	4CDZ		V	
8.1.6	Hong Hai Dan Xin	Red Ocean Red Heart	2CDZ			
8.1.7	Tao Yuan	Peach Garden	3CDZ			
8.1.8	Lan Feng Zhan Chi	Blue Phoenix Spreading Wings	2CDZ	E	V	
8.1.9	Lan Hai Ying Yue	Blue Sea Reflecting the Moon	2CDZ			
8.1.10	Tao Yun Yin Ge	Peach Garden Silver Pavilion	5CFH			
8.1.11	Lan He Dian Yun	Blue Lotus Speckled Colour	4CFH			
8.1.12	Lan Tian	Blue Sky	3CDZ			
8.2.1	Jin Ye Fen	Gold Leaf Pink	4CDZ			
8.2.2	Du Juan Ti Xue	Cuckoo's Sad Tears	3CDZ			
8.2.3	Fen Rong Cha Cui	Pink Complexion Emerald Inlay	4CDZ			
8.3.1	Liu Chun	Beautiful Spring	1CDZ			
8.3.2	Lan Hai	Blue Sea	2CDZ			
8.3.3	Lan Fu Rong	Blue Hibiscus	3CDZ			
8.3.4	Jin Yu Xi Shui	Gold Fish Playing	2CDZ			S
8.3.5	Wu Long Jiao Hai	Black Dragon Overturns the Sea	3CD			
8.4.1	Mo Shu Shi	Magician	2CDZ			
8.4.2	San Hua Nu	Girl Spreading Flower Petals	2CDZ	E	V	
8.4.3	Lan Zhen Zhu	Blue Pearl	2CDZ			
8.4.4	Lan E Rong	Blue Goose-down	3CDZ			
8.5.1	Lan Shan Hu	Blue Reef	3CDZ			
8.5.2	Lan Guan Yu Zhu	Blue Crown Jade Pearl	3CDZ		V	
8.5.3	Lan Ta Xiang Cui	Blue Pagoda Emerald Inlay	5CFH			
9.1.1	Xue Hai Fei Hong	Snow Sea Arching Rainbow	3CDZ			
9.1.2	Fen He Dian Yun	Pink Lotus Speckled Colour	3CDZ			
9.1.3	Xin He Ying Ri	New Lotus Reflecting the Sun	4CDZ			
9.1.4	Long Yuan Xia Nu	Martial Arts Girls on Gansu Plateau	4CDZ			
9.1.5	Hei Hai Feng Yun	Stormy Black Ocean	3CDZ	L		
9.1.6	Zong Ban Fen He	Brown Blotch Pink Lotus	3CDZ			
9.1.7	Zhou Lang	Handsome Mr. Zhou*	2CDZ			
9.1.8	Hei Rui Die	Black Butterfly	4CDZ	L		
9.1.9	He Tang Ying Yue	Lotus Pond Reflecting the Moon	4CDZ	L		
9.1.10	He Hua Deng	Lotus Flower Lamp	3CDZ	L		
9.1.11	Hui Die	Grey Butterfly	2CDZ	L	V	U
9.1.12	Hui He	Grey Crane	2CDZ			
9.1.13	Ri Yue Tong Hui	Sun and Moon Equal Glory	2CDZ			
9.1.14	Han Hai Bing Xin	Endless Sea Icy Heart	3CD		V	
9.2.1	Fen Bi Lan Xia	Pink Blue Cloud	4CDZ			
9.2.2	Bo Si Nu	Persian Woman	5CFH			
9.2.3	Qiao Zhuang	Disguise	3CDZ			

9.2.4	Fo Guang Lan	Buddhist-light Blue	5CFH	L		
9.2.5	Bao Lian Deng	Precious Lotus Lamp*	4CFH			
9.2.6	Wang Gong Yuan	Palace Intrigue	5CFH			
9.2.7	Qiang Wei Lan	Rose Blue	5CFH			
9.2.8	Da Mo Feng Yun	Great Desert Storm Clouds	2CDZ		V	
9.3.1	Bo Si Shao Nu	Persian Girl	3CDZ			
9.3.2	Fen Rong Su Zhuang	Pink Complexion Plain Clothes	2CDZ			
9.3.3	Chang E Ben Yue	Chang E Flying to the Moon*	2CDZ			
9.3.4	Tai Kong Ren	Astronaut	5CFH			
9.3.5	Chun You	Spring Excursion	2CDZ			
9.4.1	Fo Zhu	Buddhist Prayer Beads	2CDZ			
9.4.2	Qi Lian Zhao Hui	Qi Lian Mountain Dawn*	5CDZ			
9.4.3	Fen Zhen Zhu	Pink Pearls	5CDZ			
9.4.4	Fen Lou Dian Jin	Pink Tower Speckled Gold	3CD			
9.4.5	Yu Pan Fen Zhu	Jade Plate Pink Pearl	2CDZ			
9.4.6	He Ping Er Qiao	Peace Twin Beauties	2CDZ			
9.4.7	Feng Yan Si Qi	Smoke Rising at All Corners*	5CFH			
9.4.8	Bao Dao Shu Guang	Treasure Island Morning Light	2CDZ			
9.4.9	Man Yuan Chun Se	Garden Full of Spring Colour	2CDZ			
9.5.1	Luan Yun Fei Du	Ragged Clouds Crossing the Sky	2CDZ			
9.5.2	Gu Sha Jin Zhong	Ancient Temple Gold Bell	2CDZ			
9.5.3	Long Yuan Zhuang Shi	Heroes of Gansu Plateau	2CDZ		V	
9.5.4	Cai Lou	Coloured Pavilion	2CDZ	E		S
9.5.5	Lan Xia Fei Yun	Scudding Blue Cloud	3CD			
9.5.6	Lan Yun Qian Li	Endless Blue Clouds	3CD			
9.5.7	Cai Guan Yin Dai	Coloured Crown Silver Belt	3CD		V	S
9.5.8	Qi Lian Nong Xia	Thick Cloud on Qi Lian Mountain	3CDZ		V	
9.5.9	Cai Yun Ge	Coloured Cloud Pavilion	2CDZ			
9.5.10	Ping Fen Qiu Se	Equally Shared Autumn Colour*	2CDZ		V	U
9.5.11	Qi Lian Wan Xia	Evening Cloud on Qi Lian Mountain	5CFH			
9.5.12	Shui Man Jin Shan	Jin Mountain Submerged*	5CFH			
9.5.13	Jin Pao Yu Pei	Silk Robe Jade Belt	2CDZ			
9.5.14	Da Mo Tuo Ling	Great Desert Camel Bell*	5CFH			
9.6.1	Fen Tai Xiang Cui	Pink Tower Inlaid with Emeralds	2CDZ			
9.6.2	Lan Shan Chong Lou	Lan Mountain Pavilion Terraces	4CDZ			S
9.6.3	Xiang Yi Si Hai	Fragrance Permeates All Corners	3CDZ			
9.6.4	Er Qiao Li Xiang	Twin Beauties Idealism	5CFH			
9.6.5	He Ping Tian Shi	Peace Angel*	5CFH			

11.2 Explanatory Notes on the English Equivalent Gansu Mudan Names.

In these notes the word ancient is used loosely, not with the precise meaning it has for students of Chinese history. The terms story, legend and fairy story are used with some care but the distinctions are blurred: real characters often become the subjects of fiction.

1.1.2 See Chapter 9.2, p. 102.

1.1.5 Xue Hai, literally 'snow sea' here and in other names could mean a sea of white cloud or a range of snowy mountains like waves.

1.1.16 See Chapter 9.2, p. 102.

1.1.18 Wu Kong is the Monkey King who appears in the very famous sixteenth-century fantastical story 'Journey to the West'. The meditation here is more a reflection on his life, during a five hundred year confinement with his body, but not his head, trapped under a mountain.

1.1.19 Literally 'bear cat'.

1.1.26 Yan and Huang are legendary ancestors for the Chinese people and Huang He, the Yellow River, their legendary birthplace.

1.1.28 A familiar Chinese emblem.

1.1.31 A famous panda in Beijing Zoo.

1.1.36 A character called Guan Yu with a luxuriant beard in the ancient martial arts story 'Romance of Three Kingdoms'. Written during the Ming Dynasty and set in the pre-dynasty period of Chinese History, this is said to be the most popular historical novel in Asia

1.1.37 An idiom: a team of like-minded people working together.

1.1.38 From 'Romance of the Three Kingdoms' (see 1.1.36): in a plan devised by Zhuge Liang (see 1.1.49), straw effigies in boats are used to capture the enemy's arrows.

1.1.42 The planets of the solar system are traditionally called stars, as in the West Venus is called the morning star. The Earth Star is Saturn.

1.1.44 Zhao Jun is one of the four women in Chinese ancient history whose beauty is legendary. All four appear in Gansu Mudan names. See also 4.3.4, 4.5.9, 4.6.21.

1.1.45 The familiar stellar constellation (called the 'Cradle' in China).

1.1.49 Zhuge Liang, the master strategist in 'Romance of Three Kingdoms', is usually pictured carrying a feather fan and with his hair tied in a braid.

1.2.1 Fairy-like girls on a celestial platform in an ancient story.

1.2.2 Ji Gong's shabby palm-leaf fan. See 1.2.4.

1.2.4 The narrow base of the blotches resembles the fan carried by Ji Gong in traditional pictures. He was a legendary Buddhist wandering helper of the poor, also called the mad monk, and was said to have magical powers.

1.2.5 Yu Tang Chun is the eponymous heroine of a seventeenth-century novel.

1.2.10 Previously warring ancient (pre-dynasty) states now reconciled. Suggested by the blotch consisting of two distinct halves.

1.2.12 A big lake in Qinghai Province between Gansu and Tibet.

1.2.13 Romantic folk music because Mandarin ducks habitually go about in male and female pairs.

1.2.14 See Chapter 9.2, p. 101.

1.2.15 The treasure is the supporting pillar of the Emperor's Palace under the sea and is stolen by the Monkey King. See Chapter 9.2, p. 101.

1.2.16 An idiom-like phrase signifying health and vitality.

1.3.4 Actually the name of the twentieth of the

twenty-four solar terms (little seasons) in the Chinese calendar: round about second half of November. The twenty-first solar term is called Big Snow.

1.3.7 From a fairy tale in which a child makes a dangerous mountain journey to find a lotus flower to save his mother's life.

1.3.12 From 'Romance of the Three Kingdoms' (see 1.1.36): an account of an actual battle, the blood of the fallen coloured the river.

1.3.14 From an incident in 'Journey to the West' (see 1.1.18) in which one of the Monkey King's companions is tricked into carrying a magic fan which gets bigger and bigger.

1.3.17 A Zorro-like character from an ancient martial arts story.

1.3.19 Li Hua is the name of the heroine in a folk play traditional to Gansu.

1.4.3 Xing Long is a famous mountain in Gansu, visible from Peace Peony Nursery.

1.5.4 As the flowers age, the stamens suggest baited fishing lines. In an ancient story wise old Jiang gives the emperor advice but not directly, dropping hints to tempt the emperor's interest.

1.5.5 Gold City here refers to Lanzhou in the Han Dynasty, the capital city of Gansu.

1.6.3 A phrase from a poem in a particular form by Mao Zedong entitled Snow and describing the snowy landscapes of northern China.

1.6.7 Literally Five Gold Flowers, the name of a famous old film about five girls from a district in Yunnan where all the girls are called Gold Flowers.

1.6.13 Bai He is a lily (lilium), eaten as a vegetable, common in Gansu but a delicacy in other places.

1.6.15 White Pagoda Hill is a famous picturesque feature in Lanzhou City, Gansu.

2.1.10 Huang Shan, Yellow Mountain, is a very beautiful world heritage site in Anhui Province.

4.1.6 An idiom: literally very happy very excited and carefree.

4.1.12 An idiom: literally iron face selfless, a reference to Bao Gong, (see 6.1.7).

4.2.3 From an ancient legend, a celestial platform or stage from which a commander addresses his troops or on which ministers gather for conferences.

4.2.5 An incident from 'Journey to the West' (see 1.1.18) involving the prankster Ne Zha.

4.2.6 A traditional tableau in festivals.

4.3.2 An idiom: literally put on theatrical makeup to go on stage; in practice, somebody preparing themselves for a performance or demonstration in the theatre of life.

4.3.4 Wen Jun, from the West Han Dynasty, was one of the four legendary beauties. She was also very talented. Her story involves a romance with an eminent man of letters.

4.3.8 As 1.5.5.

4.4.2 See Chapter 9.2, p. 101.

4.4.10 From the famous eighteenth-century (Qing Dynasty) novel 'Dream of Red Chambers'. Autumn; Dai Yu sweeps fallen flower petals into a hole and feels this is a symbol for her own life.

4.5.2 Wan Li is a thousand li (about 500 km); 'Xia Guang' indicates the first rays of the sun.

4.5.7 From a fairy tale: Chang E has flown to the Moon with a white rabbit and waits for her lover.

4.5.9 Zui Fei, one of the four legendary beauties, was said to be even more attractive when slightly drunk.

4.5.20 Despite the curious name there is no story or legend involved.

4.5.21 A set phrase: an exhortation to continue learning and developing.

4.5.23 Named for Professor Li Jiajue's wife.

4.5.24 An episode from 'Journey to the West' (see 1.1.18): before the guests arrive at a party to celebrate and enjoy the ripe peaches, the Monkey King eats them.

4.6.3 Named after a Mudan scholar who visited Peace Peony Nursery for study.

4.6.10 Yu Zhong is the name of the county where Peace Peony Nursery is situated.

4.6.19 Mai Ji Shan is a mountain in Gansu.

4.6.20 Despite the curious name there is no story or legend involved.

4.6.21 As the legendary beauty, Diao Chan, bows to the Moon, a cloud discretely obscures her from the Moon's gaze.

5.5.2 Chen Hong is a famous Chinese athlete.

5.5.3 Dark coloured, named after Professor Li Jiajue.

5.5.5 The palace of Xuan Nu, a mythical person, the sister of an Emperor of the West Heaven.

6.1.1 The planet Mercury.

6.1.7 Judge Bao Gong (Bao Zheng) was a senior official of the Northern Song Dynasty and subsequently a character in ancient stories. He was highly esteemed for his strictness in upholding justice and opposing corruption no matter how powerful the miscreant. See 4.1.12 (the plants are almost identical).

6.2.5 Three prominent characters in 'Romance of the Three Kingdoms' (see 1.1.36) meet again after eighteen years.

6.3.4 A film based on a love story from the Qing Dynasty.

6.4.1 An idiom: full of life and energy prepared for anything.

6.4.17 See 4.4.10.

6.4.23 A set phrase from the time of 'The Great Leap Forward'.

6.4.26 An idiom: literally 'five colours six colours', used to describe anything that is highly coloured.

6.5.2 A set phrase: literally 'full hall red' meaning all around success, also used sarcastically to mean the opposite.

6.5.17 Literally rich beautiful red but actually combines two people's given names.

6.6.1 Here the flying swallow is not a bird but a Han Dynasty Emperor's wife.

6.6.6 Lu Mountain, in Jiangxi province, is another very beautiful mountain and world heritage site. The characters of the plant name are taken from a stanza by the famous Tang Dynasty poet Li Bai.

9.1.7 A famous heroic general from the time of the Three Kingdoms, the subject of a poem by the celebrated Song Dynasty poet Su Shi (Su Dong Po).

9.2.5 A fairy story similar to 1.3.7: here the crucial object is a lamp.

9.3.3 See 4.5.7 but here Chang E is actually making the journey.

9.4.2 Qi Lian is a mountain in Gansu.

9.4.7 A phrase from a song in a relatively modern musical pageant: an impending battle; at the four corners of the citadel smoke rises from the night watchmen's fires.

9.5.10 An idiom expressing the outcome of some sort of competitive activity in which the honours are equally shared.

9.5.12 From the epic seventeenth-century fairy story 'The Tale of the White Snake'. Also a film.

9.5.14 From far away across the (Gobi) desert the sound of a camel bell is heard.

9.6.5 A reminder that 'Peace Peony Nursery' means simply the peony nursery at the village in Gansu called Peace Village.

Paeonia Gansu Group 'Li Chun'

丽
春

MU 2005

11.3 A Basic Pronunciation Guide for *Pinyin* Cultivar Names

The main difference between words in English and words in *pinyin* is that in *pinyin* all words are essentially of one-syllable. In Chinese there are 'compound words' made up of individual *pinyin* words run together but there are none to be found in the cultivar names. The other major difference is that whereas in English the vowel sounds are simple (albeit with inconsistent and confusing spelling) and there are complicated clusters of consonants (words like 'stripe', 'fluster', 'scrounge'), in *pinyin* the consonants are simple (albeit unfamiliar in some cases) but some of the vowels are more complex sounds (e.g., 'yun' is pronounced 'yoo-un' said quickly).

A profound difficulty in the correct pronunciations of words in *pinyin* linked, in a sense, to the more complex vowels is of course the tones. There are four possible tones for most *pinyin* words: first tone - flat, second tone - rising, third tone - falling then rising, fourth tone - quick falling. Each tone usually corresponds to a substantially different meaning. For accurate pronunciation, and hence meaning each pinyin word should have the tone-marker (1,2,3 or 4) added, but as tones present a substantial extra complication, for the purposes of this basic pronunciation guide this aspect is ignored.

Most of the **consonants** in *pinyin* are pronounced as they would be commonly pronounced in English.

There are some complications with *g, z, c, zh, ch, sh, j, q, x* and *h*:

G is pronounced as in goat.
Z is pronounced like ds in adds, and C like ts in bits.

With the tongue curled back: *ZH* is pronounced similar to j in jury and ch in child.
With the tongue flat, corners of lips drawn back as far as possible: *J* is pronounced like g in genius; *Q* like ch in chew; and *SH* like sh in sheep.
X is pronounced like sh in sheep but with the lips pointing forward and corners pulled inwards.

With the back of the tongue towards the roof of the mouth: *H* is pronounced like ch in German, Rauch for example and the Scottish loch.

The **vowel** sounds are more varied. The vowels and vowel combinations that occur in Gansu Mudan names, some of which are perhaps unexpected are:

A is like a in father; *AI* like I in bite; *AO* like ow in cow, almost two vowels ah-oo.
E is like ur in fur; *EI* like ay in play; *EN* like un in under; *ENG* like ung in bung.
I (after z, c, s, zh, ch, sh and r only) is pronounced like er in wonder; elsewhere, *I* is like ea in tea.
IA is pronounced like the German ja; *IAO* like eow in meow; *IE* like ie in French Pierre; *IU* like yo in yoyo; *IAN* like Japanese yen; *IANG* like (yin and) yang; *IONG* like the German name Jung.
O is like ore in more; *OU* like o in go; *ONG* like ung in Jung;
U is like ew in stew; *UA* as in suave; *UO* is pronounced like war; *UAI* like wi in swipe; *UI* is pronounced like weigh; *UAN* like wan in wangle; *UN* like won in wondrous (but with the o like oo in book); *UANG* approximately like w-ong in wrong.
YU is like eu in pneumatic; *YUE* like eu plus air said quickly; *YUAN* like eu plus en said quickly; and *YUN* like eu plus un said quickly.

This long list of rules may seem very complicated but the magnificence of the plants deserves a little effort. And it is better to use the *pinyin* names with some errors in pronunciation than the English equivalents which should not be regarded as names at all.

Or, of course, if and when a prose name presents a problem, there is the simple and unambiguous number to use instead.

There is no accepted convention about the use of upper case with words in *pinyin*. Often upper case is used for the initial letter of each word. This has the advantage of making the individual words clearly distinct for people unfamiliar with them but seems to us generally inappropriate. However as the *pinyin* words we are concerned with are almost always proper names we have adopted the convention of initial letters in upper case.

12. CULTIVAR REFERENCE LIST

12.1 Pinyin Cultivar Names in Alphabetic Order

1.1.34	Ai	7.2.1	Da Ban Zi
1.1.47	Ao Yun Zhi Guang	9.2.8	Da Mo Feng Yun
1.3.14	Ba Jiao Shan	1.1.46	Da Mo Gu Yan
1.1.3	Bai Bi Lan Xia	9.5.14	Da Mo Tuo Ling
1.1.8	Bai He Liang Chi	4.3.6	Da Qian Shi Jie
1.6.6	Bai Pao Jin Dai	1.1.6	Da Xue Hai Bing Xin
1.6.14	Bai Xiu Qiu	4.4.10	Dai Yu Zang Hua
1.3.17	Bai Yi Da Xia	1.4.6	Dian Jin Bai Yan Wei
1.5.24	Bai Yi Nu Xia	1.1.55	Dian Jin Yan Wei Fen
1.6.10	Bai Yun Hong Xia	4.6.21	Diao Chan Bai Yue
1.5.3	Bai Zhang Bing	8.2.2	Du Juan Ti Xue
9.4.8	Bao Dao Shu Guang	4.2.6	Er Long Xi Zhu
6.1.7	Bao Gong	9.6.4	Er Qiao Li Xiang
9.2.5	Bao Lian Deng	1.3.2	Fei Tian
6.3.18	Bao Shi Lan	4.5.21	Fei Xiang Yu Zhou
1.1.45	Bei Dou Xing	4.6.24	Fei Yan Gui Chao
1.6.3	Bei Guo Feng Guang	9.2.1	Fen Bi Lan Xia
1.1.39	Bei Ji Guang	1.5.2	Fen Bi Sheng Hui
1.3.10	Bei Ji Hu	4.1.2	Fen Chi Ying Yue
1.1.22	Bei Ji Xiong	1.1.48	Fen Die Chu Yu
2.5.3	Bing Shan Cang Yu	1.5.25	Fen Ge Miao Jin
1.3.16	Bing Shan Dian Yun	4.6.13	Fen Ge Piao Cai
3.5.4	Bing Shan Fei Cui	4.6.4	Fen Guan Cai Dai
1.1.1	Bing Shan Xue Lian	4.4.3	Fen Guan Cai Die
8.1.2	Bing Xin Fen Lian	1.4.11	Fen Guan Jin Zhu
6.1.10	Bing Xin Lan He	4.4.4	Fen Guan Yu Dai
7.1.6	Bing Xin Ye Guang Bei	4.1.1	Fen He
5.2.2	Bing Xin Zi	9.1.2	Fen He Dian Yun
9.2.2	Bo Si Nu	8.1.4	Fen Jin Yu Zhu
9.3.1	Bo Si Shao Nu	1.2.11	Fen Lou Cha Cui
9.5.7	Cai Guan Yin Dai	4.5.12	Fen Lou Dan Xin
9.5.4	Cai Lou	9.4.4	Fen Lou Dian Jin
9.5.9	Cai Yun Ge	1.3.3	Fen Mian Tao Sai
1.1.38	Cao Chuan Jie Jian	4.3.2	Fen Mo Deng Chang
9.3.3	Chang E Ben Yue	8.2.3	Fen Rong Cha Cui
4.5.7	Chang E Shu Xiu	9.3.2	Fen Rong Su Zhuang
5.5.2	Chen Hong Yi Hao	9.6.1	Fen Tai Xiang Cui
6.3.15	Chen Yuan Zi	4.5.1	Fen Yan Jiao
6.5.7	Cheng Xin	4.5.18	Fen Yan Wei
4.6.1	Chu E Zhan Chi	1.3.18	Fen Yu
6.4.6	Chuan Jin Dai Yin	3.5.3	Fen Yu Dian Cui
3.1.1	Chun Dao Long Yuan	4.4.5	Fen Yu San Tai
4.6.7	Chun Jiang Yan Bo	4.6.23	Fen Yu Sheng Hui
6.3.5	Chun Man Ren Jian	9.4.3	Fen Zhen Zhu
9.3.5	Chun You	6.5.4	Feng Cai

1.5.11	Feng Chu
4.5.26	Feng Guan Yu Zhu
4.6.6	Feng Juan Can Yun
5.4.1	Feng Xian
9.4.7	Feng Yan Si Qi
4.6.8	Feng Zi Xiu Se
4.3.1	Fo Guang
1.1.43	Fo Guang Fen
4.1.9	Fo Guang Hong
9.2.4	Fo Guang Lan
9.4.1	Fo Zhu
1.1.33	Fu Ai
6.5.17	Fu Li Hong
6.2.2	Gao Gan Hong
1.6.12	Gao Lou Cang Jiao
2.3.2	Gao Yuan Shen Qiu
6.4.23	Geng Shang Yi Ceng Lou
6.6.2	Gong Deng
6.2.5	Gu Cheng Xiang Hui
9.5.2	Gu Sha Jin Zhong
1.1.57	Guan Ai
6.1.4	Guang Hui Li Cheng
1.3.1	Gui Fu Ren
4.1.14	Gui Zhong Shao Fu
9.1.14	Han Hai Bing Xin
9.1.10	He Hua Deng
1.3.6	He Luo Yin Hai
9.4.6	He Ping Er Qiao
4.3.9	He Ping Fen
4.5.27	He Ping Hong
4.6.22	He Ping Hong Xiu Qiu
4.6.18	He Ping Lan
9.6.5	He Ping Tian Shi
4.3.7	He Tang Qiu Bo
9.1.9	He Tang Ying Yue
1.1.20	Hei Bai Fen Ming
1.1.27	Hei Fa Dan Xin
1.1.4	Hei Fa Nu Lang
7.1.5	Hei Feng Die
9.1.5	Hei Hai Feng Yun
1.1.14	Hei Long Tan
9.1.8	Hei Rui Die
7.4.1	Hei Tian E
7.2.2	Hei Wang Zi
7.1.2	Hei Xuan Feng
7.1.4	Hei Yuan Shuai
7.3.2	Hei Zhen Zhu
7.1.7	Hei Zhou Chou
1.3.15	Hong Ban Ju Hua Bai
1.2.3	Hong Chi Wei Bo
1.2.7	Hong Fa Mo Nu

6.5.5	Hong Guan Xiang Cui
6.4.3	Hong Guan Yin Xian
6.5.13	Hong Guan Yu Zhu
1.2.16	Hong Guang Man Mian
5.2.4	Hong Guang Ying Tian
8.1.6	Hong Hai Dan Xin
6.3.2	Hong Hai Feng Yun
5.1.2	Hong Hai Jin Dao
6.4.4	Hong Hai Qing Long
6.3.3	Hong Hai Yang
6.2.3	Hong Hai Yin Bo
4.2.4	Hong Hai Yin Lang
4.1.3	Hong Hai Yin Zhou
4.1.5	Hong Lian
6.4.2	Hong Lou Cang Jin
4.5.25	Hong Lou Dian Jin
6.6.1	Hong Lou Fei Yan
5.5.1	Hong Lou Jin Chai
6.4.17	Hong Lou Jing Meng
6.5.6	Hong Lou Wan Zhang
4.6.11	Hong Lou Yu Ding
5.1.7	Hong Qi Man Juan
6.1.3	Hong Qian Niu
2.1.7	Hong Shu Lin
5.6.1	Hong Tai Yin Ge
6.4.9	Hong Xia Man Tian
1.1.41	Hong Xia Ying Xue
4.5.17	Hong Xian Nu
4.4.8	Hong Yi Nu Lang
6.3.10	Hong Yi Shao Nu
6.3.7	Hong Yu Fan Lang
4.5.16	Hong Yun Shan
6.4.7	Hong Yun Tu Qi
6.3.6	Hong Zhen Zhu
6.5.9	Hong Zhou Chou
6.6.4	Hong Zhuang Su Guo
1.1.51	Hong Zong Lie Ma
6.3.1	Huai Nian
2.1.8	Huang He
1.5.18	Huang He Lou
2.6.1	Huang Jin Yu Zhui
2.1.1	Huang Lian
2.1.10	Huang Shan Chen Xi
2.1.9	Huang Tu Gao Yuan
2.5.2	Huang Yun
9.1.11	Hui Die
9.1.12	Hui He
1.5.16	Huo Fo Ju Shou
1.2.4	Ji Gong
1.5.4	Jiang Tai Gong Diao Yu
1.5.12	Jiao Mei

6.1.9	Nan Hai Jin Dao	4.2.7	Wan Hua Hong
4.2.5	Ne Zha Nao Hai	4.2.8	Wan Hua Zi
6.4.11	Nong Xia Man Tian	2.3.3	Wan Xue Ying Chun
2.1.4	Pan Deng	9.2.6	Wang Gong Yuan
1.1.31	Pan Pan	4.3.4	Wen Jun Xin Meng
9.5.10	Ping Fen Qiu Se	6.5.24	Wu Cai Zi Xiu Qiu
1.4.1	Qi E Wo Bing	1.6.7	Wu Duo Jin Hua
1.4.10	Qi Lian Cai Hong	1.1.9	Wu Fa Lan Dai
9.5.8	Qi Lian Nong Xia	1.1.28	Wu Jiao Xing
9.5.11	Qi Lian Wan Xia	1.1.18	Wu Kong Xiu Xing
9.4.2	Qi Lian Zhao Hui	8.3.5	Wu Long Jiao Hai
4.4.2	Qian Zi Bai Tai	6.4.26	Wu Yan Liu Se
4.3.10	Qiang Wei Fen	5.1.6	Xi Qing You Yu
9.2.7	Qiang Wei Lan	5.1.4	Xi Yang Hong
9.2.3	Qiao Zhuang	5.1.10	Xi Yu Bing Chuan
1.2.10	Qin Jin Zhi Hao	4.5.2	Xia Guang Wan Li
4.4.9	Qing Chun	4.5.3	Xia Ran Qing Shan
4.5.19	Qing Feng Wan Xia	6.6.6	Xiang Lu Zi Yan
1.2.12	Qing Hai Hu Yin Bo	6.5.15	Xiang Yan
6.5.3	Qing Si Wan Lu	9.6.3	Xiang Yi Si Hai
5.1.5	Re Lie	1.1.25	Xiao Bai Yu
1.2.6	Re Xue Qing Chun	6.3.13	Xiao Ban Lan Xiu Qiu
6.3.16	Ri Mu Gui Tuo	6.4.10	Xiao Hong Ta
9.1.13	Ri Yue Tong Hui	1.5.26	Xiao Lou Dian Yun
1.6.13	Sai Bai He	4.5.8	Xiao Xia
8.4.2	San Hua Nu	1.3.4	Xiao Xue
5.1.8	Shen Guang	2.1.5	Xiao Xue Hai Bing Xin
4.6.5	Shen Guang Yu Lu	9.1.3	Xin He Ying Ri
4.5.5	Shen Nu	1.1.40	Xin Xing
1.1.2	Shu Sheng Peng Mo	4.1.6	Xing Gao Cai Lie
9.5.12	Shui Man Jin Shan	1.5.9	Xing Guang Can Lan
6.1.1	Shui Xing	1.4.3	Xing Long Rui Xue
9.3.4	Tai Kong Ren	1.5.7	Xing Yun
4.3.3	Tan Hua Fen	1.1.19	Xiong Mao
4.6.16	Tao Hong Xiu Qiu	1.2.9	Xiu Fa Pi Jian
4.6.14	Tao Hua Nu	6.3.11	Xiu Lou Xiang Cui
6.3.4	Tao Hua Shan	5.5.5	Xuan Nu Gong
4.5.13	Tao Hua Yuan	1.1.5	Xue Hai Bing Xin
6.3.8	Tao Rong	1.1.10	Xue Hai Chen Guang
8.1.7	Tao Yuan	1.1.24	Xue Hai Dan Xin
6.5.1	Tao Yuan Chun Se	1.1.23	Xue Hai Fang Xin
4.5.24	Tao Yuan Ju Hui	9.1.1	Xue Hai Fei Hong
8.1.10	Tao Yun Yin Ge	2.1.6	Xue Hai Yin Zhen
1.6.11	Tian Gao Yun Dan	1.1.58	Xue Hua
8.1.1	Tian Jing Nu Lang	1.3.5	Xue Li Cang Jin
4.5.22	Tian Mi De Meng	4.4.7	Xue Shan Chui Yan
1.5.8	Tian Shan Ri Chu	1.3.13	Xue Shan Fei Hong
4.6.12	Tian Shan Xia Nu	1.4.2	Xue Shan Jin Ding
4.1.12	Tie Mian Wu Si	1.5.15	Xue Shan Wan Xia
1.1.37	Tong Xin Tong De	1.3.11	Xue Shan Yu Hui
1.1.42	Tu Xing	1.6.1	Xue Ye Han Yan

1.1.50	Xue Yu Zhi Huan	4.6.10	Yu Zhong Fen
1.6.4	Xue Yuan Xing Huo	1.2.13	Yuan Yang Pu
4.2.2	Xue Yuan Yu Hui	1.6.5	Yue Zhao Kun Lun
1.5.22	Xue Yuan Zao Chun	7.1.8	Zao Yuan Hong
1.3.12	Xue Zhan Chang Ban Po	1.1.44	Zhao Jun Fei Yun
6.5.10	Yan Chun	1.4.4	Zhen Zhu Bai
1.1.29	Yan Hua Chu Fang	4.4.11	Zhen Zhu Nu
1.1.26	Yan Huang Er Nu	4.5.11	Zhong Jie Mei
5.2.3	Yan Li	4.6.15	Zhong Shan Feng Yu
1.6.15	Yan Rao Bai Ta	1.1.21	Zhong Xing Peng Yue
1.4.7	Yan Wei Bai	9.1.7	Zhou Lang
1.2.1	Yao Tai Jiu Nu	6.3.14	Zhou Mei Gui
7.1.1	Ye Guang Bei	7.1.10	Zi Die Chu Yu
1.1.15	Yi Dian Mo	7.1.9	Zi Die Ying Feng
1.1.16	Yi Ding Mo	6.5.16	Zi Gong Chun Xiu
6.3.17	Yi Jie Jin Lan	6.5.26	Zi Guan Yin Xian
1.6.9	Yin Bai He	6.4.13	Zi Guan Yu Chi
1.1.30	Yin Die Fei Wu	4.6.25	Zi Guan Yu Dai
1.2.8	Yin Hai Hong Bo	6.5.12	Zi Guan Yu Zhu
1.5.17	Yin Ju Cui Rui	6.4.15	Zi Gui Yin Mai
1.3.9	Yin Lou Hui Cai	5.3.3	Zi Hai Yin Bo
1.1.35	Yin Pan Tuo Gui	6.1.6	Zi Hai Yin Guang
1.1.11	Yin Pan Zi Zhu	6.5.14	Zi Jin Cheng
1.4.15	Yin Shan Dan Xia	6.4.18	Zi Jin Guan
2.1.2	Yin Si Bai	5.1.9	Zi Jin Huan
4.6.20	Yin Xian Diao Jin Gui	6.5.18	Zi Jin Ting
1.2.2	Yin Yang Shan	5.2.1	Zi Kui Xiang Ri
1.5.19	Yin Zhuang Su Guo	5.3.1	Zi Ling Long
4.1.8	Ying Ri He Hua	6.5.19	Zi Lou Cang Yu
6.1.2	You Yi	6.5.20	Zi Lou Xiang Jin
1.5.1	Yu Ban Xiu Qiu	6.5.22	Zi Luo Yin Wei
1.1.7	Yu Feng Dian Tou	6.4.12	Zi Pao Chen Shuang
1.3.20	Yu Guan Cai Dai	6.5.21	Zi Pao Yin Bian
1.5.13	Yu Guan Hei Fa	5.4.2	Zi Ta Dian Jin
1.5.6	Yu Guan Jin Zhu	6.4.20	Zi Ta Xiang Cui
1.5.14	Yu Guan Lan Dai	7.3.1	Zi Ta Yan Yun
1.5.21	Yu Guan Xiang Cui	4.4.6	Zi Xia Dong Zhao
2.3.1	Yu Guan Yue	4.5.6	Zi Xian Nu
2.1.3	Yu He Dian Yun	6.2.4	Zi Yan
1.1.17	Yu Long Bei	8.1.3	Zi Ye Fen
1.6.2	Yu Lou Cang Jiao	5.3.2	Zi Yuan Yang
4.4.1	Yu Lou Fen	4.4.12	Zi Yun Feng
1.4.14	Yu Lou Pi Cai	6.4.21	Zi Zhen Zhu
1.5.10	Yu Lou Shan Jin	5.5.4	Zi Zhou Chou
1.5.23	Yu Lou Xiang Cui	6.4.16	Zi Zhu Lin
1.2.14	Yu Lu Lian Dan	1.1.56	Zong Ban Bai
1.3.8	Yu Nu Tan Hai	8.1.5	Zong Ban Fen
9.4.5	Yu Pan Fen Zhu	9.1.6	Zong Ban Fen He
1.1.49	Yu Shan Guan Jin	4.5.9	Zui Fei
1.2.5	Yu Tang Chun		

12.2 Chinese Character Cultivar Names

1.1.1	冰山雪莲	1.1.50	雪域之欢	1.4.5	娇玉
1.1.2	书生捧墨	1.1.51	红鬃烈马	1.4.6	点金白燕尾
1.1.3	白碧蓝霞	1.1.52	巨斑粉	1.4.7	燕尾白
1.1.4	黑发女郎	1.1.53	金丝白	1.4.8	金波荡漾
1.1.5	雪海冰心	1.1.54	金叶白	1.4.9	菊花黄
1.1.6	大雪海冰心	1.1.55	点金燕尾粉	1.4.10	祁连彩虹
1.1.7	玉凤点头	1.1.56	棕斑白	1.4.11	粉冠金珠
1.1.8	白鹤亮翅	1.1.57	关爱	1.4.12	菊花粉
1.1.9	乌发蓝带	1.1.58	雪花	1.4.13	柳腰白
1.1.10	雪海晨光	1.2.1	瑶台九女	1.4.14	玉楼披彩
1.1.11	银盘紫珠	1.2.2	阴阳扇	1.4.15	银山丹霞
1.1.12	巨荷三变	1.2.3	红池微波	1.5.1	玉瓣绣球
1.1.13	暮春白	1.2.4	济公	1.5.2	粉碧生辉
1.1.14	黑龙潭	1.2.5	玉堂春	1.5.3	百丈冰
1.1.15	一点墨	1.2.6	热血青春	1.5.4	姜太公钓鱼
1.1.16	一锭墨	1.2.7	红发魔女	1.5.5	金城明月
1.1.17	玉龙杯	1.2.8	银海红波	1.5.6	玉冠金珠
1.1.18	悟空修行	1.2.9	秀发披肩	1.5.7	星云
1.1.19	熊猫	1.2.10	秦晋之好	1.5.8	天山日出
1.1.20	黑白分明	1.2.11	粉楼插翠	1.5.9	星光灿烂
1.1.21	众星捧月	1.2.12	青海湖银波	1.5.10	玉楼闪金
1.1.22	北极熊	1.2.13	鸳鸯谱	1.5.11	凤雏
1.1.23	雪海芳心	1.2.14	玉炉炼丹	1.5.12	娇美
1.1.24	雪海丹心	1.2.15	龙宫得宝	1.5.13	玉冠黑发
1.1.25	小白玉	1.2.16	红光满面	1.5.14	玉冠蓝带
1.1.26	炎黄儿女	1.3.1	贵夫人	1.5.15	雪山晚霞
1.1.27	黑发丹心	1.3.2	飞天	1.5.16	活佛聚首
1.1.28	五角星	1.3.3	粉面桃腮	1.5.17	银菊翠蕊
1.1.29	烟花初放	1.3.4	小雪	1.5.18	黄河楼
1.1.30	银蝶飞舞	1.3.5	雪里藏金	1.5.19	银妆素裹
1.1.31	盼盼	1.3.6	鹤落银海	1.5.20	陇原雪
1.1.32	墨斑银光	1.3.7	莲花山	1.5.21	玉冠镶翠
1.1.33	父爱	1.3.8	玉女探海	1.5.22	雪原早春
1.1.34	爱	1.3.9	银楼绘彩	1.5.23	玉楼镶翠
1.1.35	银盘托桂	1.3.10	北极狐	1.5.24	白衣女侠
1.1.36	美髯公	1.3.11	雪山余辉	1.5.25	粉阁描金
1.1.37	同心同德	1.3.12	血战长板坡	1.5.26	小楼点晕
1.1.38	草船借箭	1.3.13	雪山飞虹	1.5.27	兰花女
1.1.39	北极光	1.3.14	芭蕉扇	1.6.1	雪夜寒烟
1.1.40	新星	1.3.15	红斑菊花白	1.6.2	玉楼藏娇
1.1.41	红霞映雪	1.3.16	冰山点晕	1.6.3	北国风光
1.1.42	土星	1.3.17	白衣大侠	1.6.4	雪原星火
1.1.43	佛光粉	1.3.18	粉玉	1.6.5	月照昆仑
1.1.44	昭君飞晕	1.3.19	梨花醉酒	1.6.6	白袍锦带
1.1.45	北斗星	1.3.20	玉冠彩带	1.6.7	五朵金花
1.1.46	大漠孤烟	1.4.1	企鹅卧冰	1.6.8	昆仑秋色
1.1.47	奥运之光	1.4.2	雪山金顶	1.6.9	银百合
1.1.48	粉蝶初羽	1.4.3	兴隆瑞雪	1.6.10	白云红霞
1.1.49	羽扇纶巾	1.4.4	珍珠白	1.6.11	天高云淡

Paeonia Gansu Group 'Yan Wei Bai'

燕
尾
白